Mapping DRAMA

CREATING, DEVELOPING & EVALUATING PROCESS DRAMA

Mapping Drama focuses on creating practical drama structures and developing process drama. It explores realistic and effective methods of reflecting on, assessing and evaluating work in drama to ensure progress. At the core of the book sit seven pretexts that have been used and continue to be used to generate drama and theatre which engages, challenges and excites groups of all ages and abilities.

ALLAN OWENS & KEITH BARBER

Allan Owens is a Senior Lecturer in Drama and Theatre Studies at Chester College of Higher Education. He has worked in secondary schools, further education and the advisory service. He currently teaches on B.A., M.A., B.Ed., M.Ed., P.G.C.E. (Secondary Drama) courses and is an OFSTED Inspector for drama. Through this work he continues to practise drama education in school, college, prison and the wider community both in this country and abroad.

Keith Barber is Head of Lower School at The Queen Katherine School, Kendal, Cumbria. He has taught drama in a wide range of secondary schools, rural and inner-city. Before moving to his present post he was Head of Drama in a community school for eight years which involved working with a wide range of ages and abilities. His work currently involves him in teaching drama in partnership primary schools.

Dedication
To : Our Dads and Mums, Clare, Kaz, April, Rosie, Jasmine, Mattie & Susie.

Acknowledgments
We owe much to a whole host of writers on drama which we hope is adequately acknowledged in the text and illustrative booklist.

This book represents our personal view of drama but this has inevitably been shaped by particular individuals and groups. Whilst they cannot and may not want to be held responsible for the work, we would like to gratefully acknowledge their encouragement and influence. Direct references are given in the form of end notes.

Published by Carel Press Ltd, 4 Hewson Street, Carlisle, Tel 01228 538928
info@carelpress.co.uk   www.carelpress.co.uk
© 2001 Allan Owens & Keith Barber
Cover and inside design: Flip-Side Design 01555 660091
Printed by Ashford Colour Press Ltd.

Environmental Information
The book is printed on 100% recycled paper which is made entirely from printed waste, & is not re-bleached. Using recycled paper saves trees, water & energy, & reduces air pollution & landfill.

British Library Cataloguing in Publication Data
Owens, Allan
Mapping Drama: creating and evaluating drama
1. Drama - Study and teaching
I. Title   II. Barber, Keith
792.071
ISBN 1-872365-65-5

CONTENTS

Mapping Drama offers a framework for the practitioner to reflect on and evaluate process drama. It is essential reading for all those using or teaching drama: specialists and non-specialists, students, lecturers and practitioners interested in process drama.

Our previous publication, Dramaworks, looks in depth at planning, creating and developing drama pretexts.

INTRODUCTION

In **Mapping Drama** we reflect on what makes process drama work and consider ways of evaluating and developing practice.

Many years ago we stumbled upon a book called 'The Walkers Handbook'. It included chapters on: 'Planning a walk and map reading', 'Behaviour in the countryside', 'Challenging walks', and 'How to make a diversion and still stay on course'[1]. It was a book of reference written with the novice walker in mind but intended to also be useful for the more experienced. Three points came across strongly:

- to enjoy the great outdoors certain preparations prior to the walk are essential.
- during the walk the decisions you make should be based on a careful assessment of the context you find yourself in regardless of prior plans.
- looking at the map after the walk lets you re-visit scenes and sites from a comfortable position and provides the opportunity to begin to plan the next walk.

Mapping Drama is written in the same spirit but focuses on the great indoors. In it we identify the preparations and considerations that are made when we create, develop, evaluate and assess process drama. A framework for planning and evaluating drama is presented in the form of a series of questions. In asking these questions we 'map' our way through the landscapes of imagination created in process drama, hence the title of this book.

In the text we refer to the teacher / leader of a process drama as the 'practitioner'. This is to signal that the work has taken place in other contexts as well as schools, for example in prisons and community centres. In such places the word teacher is sometimes inappropriate. Having said this, the examples we give of practice are almost exclusively from school settings. We believe most practitioners will be able to relate to this context. We have also preserved the phrase 'teacher in role' as this refers directly to a well documented form of work. In the text of this book, when referring to the practitioner we have used 'he' and 'she' in equal amounts. This has been done to avoid a gender imbalance which would go against the spirit of the work.

As ever, we detail a number of pretexts [2] which we have made work. Each has been amended and changed many times in the light of reflection on experience. We strongly believe that, in a book for the practitioner, offering theory without practice is not acceptable, at least not on a cold and wet January day when faced with a long session and a challenging group.

DEVELOPING AND EVALUATING OUR PRACTICE

When we use pretexts we assume that the drama structure created can and should be used again with different groups in different contexts. We also assume that by deconstructing a session we can adapt and improve a pretext. This section of the book is presented as a series of questions to which a range of answers are given. These can aid reflection and are helpful considerations in planning and creating work.

The questions are arranged under a number of headings:
Contract, investment and ownership,
Learning outcomes and aims,
Role,
Situation,
Focus, tension, symbol & metaphor,
Conventions,
Quality of intervention,
Questioning,
External factors.

Examples from practical work are given under each heading to provide a clear context, a concrete grounding, for what at times might appear to be abstract concepts. Some of the examples are drawn from work on pretexts in this book, others from different pretexts.

CONTRACT, INVESTMENT AND OWNERSHIP

Was the Drama Contract established and re-negotiated?

A drama contract arises 'when a practitioner and a group enter into an agreement to do something on mutually agreed and binding terms.' When we first meet a group we negotiate a contract. This gives both the leader and the participants the right to 'stop the drama' and work out together why it is not working and what needs to be done to make it work. One of the big virtues of a contract is that it is impersonal and negotiated before conflict starts, so if conflict occurs you are not locked in to a personal 'I told you to do...and you refused' head to head argument. It is just a breach of contract - no argument, no personal recrimination. With a contract you have a strategy to move forward when the process is not working.

There is nothing wrong in stopping a drama session. In the primary classroom and with community groups it is relatively easy to switch to another activity. With an older group you may have to revert to an activity you know they will engage in e.g. small group play making or games. With young children you may try to build up the time you spend doing drama starting from just five minutes. It is often counter-productive to move into the hall and feel you have to fill an hour regardless of the level of the group's development. Drama is a demanding activity. It is often better to feel that you are succeeding for 5 minutes rather than failing for 45 minutes.

It is perhaps helpful to think of contracts in drama as short term and long term. The length of a long term contract can be defined as the period of time that the group and teacher are all going to be working together. For example, in a secondary school this may well be over a two year 'A' Level Course. In a primary school it could be for the year that the teacher and class are together, in a community group for the whole length of the project or course. This contract would detail how we wanted to work together and would examine how we wanted our working relationship to develop. This could be written up and put up on the classroom or studio wall or could be simply a verbal agreement.

In a lecture at an NATD conference [3], 'The Fight For Drama, The Fight For Education' Dorothy Heathcote listed a number of paradigms - ways in which teachers perceived their working relationship with a class:

Child as Flower given enough time and care, you will grow
Child as Candle You can rely on me to keep you lit up
Child as Echo No! do it the way I've said / shown you
Child as Friend If I am nice to you will you.....?
Child as Adversary The trouble with you lot (class) is....
Child as Clay In time you'll turn into the class I want
Child as Crucible Me and you have to keep stirring everything around
Child as Machine By October they should be able to....
Child as Vessel We did towns yesterday, today we are going to do....

As practitioners we all, at times, slip into using many or most of these paradigms. Heathcote emphasised that she saw 'Child as Adversary' as a destructive paradigm which must be avoided at all times. She saw 'Child as Crucible' as the most healthy paradigm for learning to take place. We once read these paradigms out to a group and briefly explained what each one meant. We then went over the list again and asked them to say "yes" if they felt we had ever reacted to them in that way.

They reacted to most of the list, perhaps suggesting that as practitioners we will try all methods during a session. Different individuals reacted positively to different paradigms, disagreeing strongly with some of their peers.

A contract may well be with a whole group, but as practitioners we must constantly be aware that we are dealing with a group of individuals who may well have interpreted the contract in very different ways. Like Heathcote we would hope to base our relationship on the idea of 'stirring things around together' but knowing that leader and group members can work together or autonomously as the process requires. Some individuals or groups may hold you as their adversary. If they want this, then the long term contract cannot meaningfully or constructively be made at this stage.

Future re-negotiations would have to occur until a mutually satisfactory agreement was reached. This would tie in with aims, objectives, and assessment where relevant. Also in a long term contract we would set achievable goals, stating where we thought we could be at the end of a time period.

By **short term contract** we mean one or two sessions. The main role of a short term contract is to give individuals ownership of their drama. If they do not believe that the drama belongs to them then the scope for learning is reduced. Ownership comes when the pupils believe that they are making decisions that directly affect the direction and focus of the drama and that their views are valued. This does not mean that we cannot challenge. As each challenge is considered, more commitment can result. The importance of the whole concept of ownership is illustrated in this example.

I had always believed in the importance of ownership, but the following incident early in my career really brought home to me the power of pupil ownership. As teacher in charge of drama in a secondary school I felt under two pressures, the first was to produce schemes of work that could be presented to an outside body, and the second was to provide some concrete help for fairly inexperienced teachers. Both of these pressures resulted in the drawing up of a year seven scheme of work which included a half term (seven week) block following a project called 'The Way West' as outlined in Drama Structures by Cecily O'Neill and Alan Lambert[4] (Hutchinson 1975). This looked fairly interesting and presented inexperienced teachers with clear content materials and ways of working.

I presented this project to my own Year Seven group, and we commenced work. After two lessons the project was obviously failing, the quality of the work was very average and the main problem seemed to be that the pupils had no enthusiasm or interest. I stopped the session and asked them to evaluate their work, they said they felt it was very poor. With further discussion it turned out that they had no interest whatsoever in what they were doing. They had not chosen to look at 'The Way West.' As it was my choice I needed to invest it with enthusiasm and importance. I had failed to do this because, if I was honest with myself, I did not have any enthusiasm for the subject either.

The pupils had now thoroughly lost any vestige of ownership in the work, and were simply going through the motions, the possibility for learning had now evaporated. We stopped work and tried to negotiate a meaningful way forward.

We found one, they wanted to do Gang Warfare! Thinking on my feet I played a game with them called Tee-ak-ee-allio, a competitive team game which gives group identity and the sense of opposition to another group.[5]

From here I asked them to find a name for their group, a costume, build a base, and devise a movement piece which told us about their gang. For the next lesson they brought in music and costume, and the whole atmosphere was completely different. They were excited about the work and I felt the commitment was total. Briefly, the work then progressed to a symbolic confrontation, and the module finished with a debriefing on the consequences of this confrontation. We became the parents of the gang members, involved members of society such as the police, and met to see if we could find out the cause of this violence. We than became experts who were given the brief of finding a solution to the problem of bored youths. This was then applied to the situation in our own area.

We could have flogged on along the Oregon Trail, but that would have been pointless - I had failed to make a mutually acceptable contract with the group. Instead the pupils gained ownership in the work, and the resulting commitment lead to the possibility of a real learning situation.

This example may seem to run against the whole concept of using pretexts which is put forward in this book. We believe that any mechanistic, spiritless following of any drama structure will produce poor work which nobody cares about because nobody owns it. The point we are making is that the pretext of 'The Oregon Trail' was used in such a formulaic way that the individuals were not being given the chance to make any real decisions. Situations were arising, the outcome was known and the group were simply led through the pretext because the practitioner had no personal interest or investment in content or form of this pretext. In the hands of someone who had all these things the resultant drama could have been excellent. Interest in the subject would have allowed the teacher to invest energy and enthusiasm in the pretext, which in turn would have had much more of a chance of gaining commitment. This in turn would have led to a level of ownership which made belief a possibility.

One last point needs to be clarified in terms of contract and ownership. We believe that the practitioner has a clear responsibility for enabling a group to progress, but can not 'do' this on a group's behalf. Pretexts can be presented as scaffolding structures for drama work but it is the group that develops work from these. It is not the drama practitioner's job to provide an endless stream of ideas in terms of form and content for any group. As in any good teaching and learning practice, the ultimate goal is autonomy, independence and mutual respect.

LEARNING OUTCOMES AND AIMS

What was the drama about? Did you know? Did the group know?

At the beginning of any drama session it is important for the practitioner to share or negotiate with the group possible learning outcomes that may occur in or through the drama. This will usually be done as part of the contract but is not in itself the learning contract.

We usually seek to highlight several outcomes at the start of a pretext. We will use the 'Dirty Clothes' pretext (page 38) as an example.

Learning Outcomes

Participants will be given the opportunity to

1 **Drama & Theatre Specific skills and knowledge**
   demonstrate an awareness of focus and tension
   control movement and voice to suggest a quality rather than literal representation
2 **Social Skills**
   learn about empathy
   learn respect for other cultures and views of reality
3 **Possible Learning Areas**
   learn about human rights and cruelty to children
   learn about animals and human friendship

These are only possible learning outcomes. As practitioners we may be particularly concerned with the skill of managing tension or the learning area of assertiveness. In the course of the long drama project which is started by a pretext, many more or different outcomes may become relevant and will be explicitly acknowledged and highlighted. We believe that by making this framework explicit, individuals can recognise and determine what they are learning both in and through drama, the two strands being inextricably intertwined. The pretext provides a scaffolding structure which allows the group to focus on and choose the area that most interests and engages them. This often relates to their specific context. For example:

One group working with the pretext 'Dirty Clothes' asked if it was realistic to believe that no one in a village would do anything if they believed or even knew that a child was being badly treated. This led to various personal stories being told about such situations. One woman said that she had lived next door to a family where she knew such a situation was going on for two years. She desperately wanted to do something but every time she asked the youngster if everything was all right she was told in no uncertain terms that it was and she should mind her own business. Should she have acted differently? What if she had interfered and matters had become worse?

A range of other stories were told about how it is possible today to live in a flat or street and not know, or even recognise, your neighbours. This specific context obviously had a resonance for this group and the pretext developed in the direction of an exploration of 'bystander apathy'; why some people intervene and others do not when they see cruelty towards children. In this particular case, the first story told was used as a basis for some forum theatre based on the individual's careful reconstruction of the scenario described.

On another occasion a group starting from the same pretext quickly decided that they would like to turn their work on it into a piece of theatre in education which they performed and workshopped with younger pupils in the school. In their developed scenario the opening of the story was the same as in the pretext, presented through action and narration to an audience but time was spent on issues of presentation. The animals from the north American village of many years ago flew through time to the present-day town where the school was based, on a mission to seek advice from people who lived there.

These two, and many other, developments were launched from the original pretext. That is the function of a pretext, to allow the group to make meaning according to the needs, wants and purposes they feel are important. Pretexts are liberating rather than reductive and restrictive. Because this is the case, all three areas of learning outcomes can only be listed as 'possible'. As the work progresses so the focus shifts in response to the contextual subtext [6] chosen by the group in negotiation with the practitioner. Contextual subtext is defined as the connecting point/s individuals in a group make with either the content or form of material being explored.

Aims

We use the term aims to refer to the practitioner's aspirations for the session. They fall into two categories.

Her aims for the group
a   The whole group eg stop allowing the boys/males to dominate discussion and make more demands of others.
b   Individuals eg for 'Alison Page' to sustain a role for more than one minute. Her aims for herself eg improve questioning techniques, take more risks with teacher in role.

It may or may not be appropriate for these aims also to be shared with the group. This depends on timing and the current relationship with them.

When a pretext is refined and rewritten in the light of experience with many groups, some of the learning outcomes and aims become very well honed and focused. At the same time the structure of the pretext develops more possibilities of opening up new learning outcomes.

If learning outcomes and aims are not clarified and shared as appropriate with the group when launching work, then confusion over purpose can seriously impede progress. For example if when starting using the 'Dirty Clothes' pretext, the practitioner did not make it clear to an older group that she was only looking for a control of movement and voice to suggest a quality rather than a literal presentation, individuals could feel very embarrassed when they first had to respond in 'animal roles'. On the other hand, another group could feel very cheated if they were not allowed to create the animals as fully as possible in order to represent them in performance. If any of these situations were not clarified, the practitioner could have one set of expectations and the group another. This ordering and sharing of priorities allows the drama to function with purpose.

It is healthy and a natural part of the creative process to live with a degree of uncertainty, but in a social and collective art form such as drama it is essential for the group to share an understanding about their general direction at any given moment. Discussing aims, and how to achieve them, from the outset allows a marker to be put down at the start of the journey. The aims may change later according to their needs, wants and purposes and can be reflected upon during evaluation.

ROLE

Were roles clearly established?

Once the contract has been made, the landscape of the drama needs to be agreed upon. In order to do this four aspects need establishing:

- role – who we are
- situation – where we are
- focus – what is at the centre of the action as the drama starts
- tension – which often comes from perspective i.e. past history of events up to the moment of encounter.

Let's deal with the first of them, **role**.

Taking on a role involves adopting an attitude [7] which may be either your own, or another based on someone else's, or be a composite. The attitude may be very different from, even the reverse of, the one that participants usually have in everyday life. The purpose of this is not initially to act out a character that can be read by others, but to use a range of attitudes to engage with the subject being explored.

The participants must also be able to enter comfortably into the imaginary situation. An inexperienced group may need protecting into role. Simply to ask them to 'be' someone, without paying attention to context, can be disastrous. We believe strongly in using all of the methods and strategies available to us as drama practitioners to offer this protection. Our practice is eclectic. However, we also believe that, for us, one of the most powerful ways of launching work is through whole group improvisation, with the practitioner in role. This is a key convention which allows the practitioner to challenge, support and develop the drama and individual contributions, from within the drama. This has to be dramatically appropriate and used for a purpose. It allows you to present stereotypes with an irony yet sufficient seriousness of intent to encourage participants to challenge, question, consider the implications of accepting the attitude being presented and make decisions. For example when teacher in role is hot seated as the hunter in 'Dirty Clothes' he can be presented as a bigot and chauvinist. If it is made clear through signals from the practitioner in role that challenges are going to be relished then the tension grows.

For example, 'Were you loved as a child?' was asked by one individual in response to the hunter's statement that, 'Children need to know fear if they are to survive'.

The participants must have a clear role, as must the leader. For the leader's role to be successful many factors must be considered. For example: A practitioner entering into role needs to be aware of the status of that role. Participants are usually very aware of the leader in a drama session. The chosen status of the role that the leader adopts, high or low, can determine largely how the participants will react within the drama. Both could be equally valid if the leader was looking for a certain reaction at a certain time to move the drama forwards. However, what is important is that the practitioner is aware of the possible consequences the choice of status could have.

Numerous publications have been written which provide a clear insight to the issue of status of teacher in role, including status [8]. Not surprisingly, the categories of high/middle/low are used to describe basic alternatives. Within this there are variations depending on intent. The function of teacher in role is usually seen as not simply an enabler but as an active shaper and challenger within the work. There is no formula to say what is exactly appropriate at a given time. This is where the skill and artistry of the leader and participants comes in to play.

One consideration is how to achieve this status. Register is the way in which you relate to and use language to converse with other participants when in role. For example you could adopt the register of sharer of information, authority figure, innocent questioner, provocateur, pointer of consequences, dogsbody, provider etc. Register is, in essence, the way you relate to pupils when in role.

The best way of arriving at an understanding of this is perhaps by trying out some of the many variations. Here is one example:

I was working in the 'provider' register. I was working with a group of fifteen and sixteen year olds on a project set in the future. They were in role as a group of adolescents who had been together since birth. They had been kept in a kind of home, totally cut off from the rest of society with which they had had no contact at all. The only education they had received was from a computer screen. When they switched roles to the organisers of this home, they decided that the experiment was now proving too expensive and abandoned the project. The children were to be moved out to an ex-army camp where they were to make their own way.

Back in role as the children, the teenagers were taken to the camp, shown some buildings and told to make their homes in them. They were told to ask for anything they needed from the stores. As the storekeeper I was adopting the register of 'provider', a sort of shadowy/fringe role. Simply by giving out a very unequal distribution of wealth the drama really took off. A group with a strong sense of identity collapsed, and conflict and division ensued. This was a group of teenagers who were anxious about leaving school and going into the world of work, and this session provided valuable discussion about how well prepared they were and what they still needed to find out.

Role, status and register must be appropriate, they should be carefully considered before the practitioner involves herself in the drama.

Once the practitioner has decided on role, status and register, how does she achieve these? The answer lies in careful attention being paid to verbal and non-verbal signals [9]. It is not just what you say, but how you say it and the physical position you adopt. Creating an effective role can be a matter of chance, but through trial and error along with constant personal evaluation, a practitioner will develop the skill of adopting the right role at the right time, with significant consequences for the quality of learning. We said earlier that adopting a role is different from acting in a naturalistic sense where the aim is to represent a credible, created character. In this sense the skills of the traditionally trained actor could be useful or detrimental to the drama depending on how they are used.

The emphasis in this section so far has been upon the use of role in spontaneous encounters. Of course this does not mean that later on in the work time could not be spent in exploring and preparing for a performance of some aspect of the work. If, for example, a naturalistic presentation was fixed upon, time would naturally be spent on characterisation. What it does mean is that in the initial stages such intentions are secondary to the group's joint exploration of an agreed focus. The learning emphasis at this stage is on each individual's personal understanding, attitudes, values and beliefs in relation to those of others.

The session about to be described also illustrates two other factors when working in role, these are partnership in role [10] and prepared roles. Partnership in role occurs when the leader is working together with a partner whose function is to act as a live focus within the drama. Working with another person in role can be very rewarding, especially if it is someone with some drama experience. If another experienced leader is not available, we often try to include interested adults, members of the community or ex-pupils. This group of 15-16 year olds was looking at the subject of the First World War [11]:

Out of role, the workshop leader began by making the contract, recognising the difficulties of a strange situation, and explaining that we would be working in a way with which they were familiar. He then told them that they were going to be volunteers, going over to France to treat the wounded from the trenches. He said they would receive basic first aid training and would need to pass a basic examination. He then went into role as their instructor and began to train them. They were taught such things as artificial respiration, how to deal with burns, how to stem bleeding, and how to apply bandages and slings.

Slowly the pupils' role was being teased out and they began to discover an attitude as they practised on each other. It was then announced that a dignitary, Lady Macmillan, would be visiting the next day to witness their examination and distribute certificates to the successful candidates. The day of the test arrived, tension was mounting all the time, and each pupil was put through an examination of their practical skills.

They all passed and were presented with badges and certificates. They then listened to a speech from Lady Macmillan, designed to make them feel proud, patriotic and ready to do their best for their country.

Lady Macmillan was a prepared role carried out by a teacher who was in period costume and who signalled her trust and pride in them using carefully considered vocabulary. By now the pupils' role had deepened, they were adopting the attitude of feeling patriotic, prepared and proud of their achievements. The badges had become important to them and were later to prove symbolic.

News arrived that four lorry loads of wounded were expected within twelve hours. They had that long to set up their field hospital. They defined the space within the drama studio, setting up specialist areas within the hospital and deciding upon specialist roles amongst themselves. Tension mounted as the approach of the wounded neared, this was aided by teacher in role comments such as 'I can see the convoy now, they're about two miles away.'

Tension had reached a climax as the pivotal point of the drama was reached, in walked a German officer, announcing he had eighty badly wounded soldiers in need of immediate treatment. There followed a silence, a powerful dramatic moment. They eventually told the German officer that they must have time to decide what they were going to do.

He left to give them time to discuss the situation, returning at an appropriate moment to tell them that four of his men had died whilst they were making up their minds what to do. Eventually the participants polarised into two camps, the conflict between their humanitarian and patriotic instincts was intense. Every conceivable argument was put forward from each side. One group decided to send for the wounded, the other group said they would rather leave than treat the enemy. The first group said they were not fit to wear the badge of a first aider and demanded that they remove their badges. They refused. At this point we stopped the drama.

Evaluation was long and debriefing was done slowly and carefully, emotions needed to be talked through. As a group of practitioners, we then needed time to evaluate pupil performance, so the pupils then elected to carry on by re-forming the group at a reunion dinner some ten years after the war was over.

Careful setting up of role was central to the success of this drama. The pupils' role was clear and they were given time to establish it. Passing the examination and being presented with a badge took a long time, but were crucial in establishing belief in the role. Each of the practitioners' roles was very carefully thought out, to the finest of details. The role of the German officer had been conveyed by carefully chosen items of uniform. His posture had been of someone who was himself wounded and very tired, and his status was that of someone who was both responsible and desperate. The practitioners were not relying upon acting skills, but their 'performances' owed much to the conventions of the theatre - the timing of the German officer's entrance was crucial. Stance and status, created by signals arising from voice, posture and costume all created the roles to achieve a challenging and stimulating drama session.

SITUATION

Was the situation clearly established?

Situation is the 'where' of the drama. Situation may well be established before role, focus and tension, but it is a major factor whatever the order.

It is not the space itself that is so important, though it may restrict certain activities, but what the practitioner does with the space available. If the space is not defined by mutual agreement difficulties can easily arise on many levels. For example, from our long term contract pupils in a school may have a clear understanding of how they use space in the drama studio. They must walk in quietly, girls change in the changing room, boys in the studio. When they are ready they sit quietly on the floor and wait until we are all ready. There are certain 'no go areas', eg behind the curtains, and work must only occur on the wooden floor area, not on the raised seating.

On another level, the way the 'aesthetic space' [12] is created and used can be critical in ensuring quality drama work. This can be thought of in long term and short term approaches. A meaningful use of space in the long term will create a place where a group wants to come and wants to learn. This could be a purpose built drama studio or equally a re-arranged general purpose room. Once defined, the drama space can have a special atmosphere for the group. We try to create a place where they feel safe and cared for, somewhere they can say things that they would not elsewhere and know that these statements stay in the space. This is a process of mutual trust and has to be developed carefully. The way you greet a group, for instance, is crucial. Whenever possible, we like to stand at the door and have a quiet chat with some of them before they get changed. This will be a serious and calm discussion, or even just a one word greeting, setting the tone for the rest of the lesson. For good drama work to occur the space must be a special place, 'an educational space' [13] where extraordinary things can happen. Even the ritual of moving chairs and tables to the side of the room and sitting on the floor in a circle can create such a space.

In the short term, the space can be drastically altered in lots of ways. It should still remain that safe place, but lesson by lesson it can be altered to produce a different dynamic. One of the quickest and most effective ways to define space and create atmosphere is through the use of simple lighting and sound. For example, once when we had spent time re-arranging the lights and playing a chosen soundtrack to create an eerie atmosphere for a project on the supernatural, one particularly disruptive pupil said as he entered, 'I can tell it's going to be good today.' The creation of atmosphere by simply defining the space had hooked his interest immediately.

Many practitioners do not have the luxury of purpose-built facilities, but some go to extraordinary lengths, when setting up their space, to create a whole environment. They sometimes do this alone, sometimes with some of the group prior to the session, sometimes with the whole group at the start of the session. Such effort can engage and excite the participants. Their imagination is already at work as they arrange or build. A commitment is being given and belief is already being built. Blacking out the space, using an overhead projector as a light source and CD/tape player can build levels of expectation.

Once the session has begun, it is important to define the space to everybody's satisfaction. Everyone must have a clear idea of where everything is. 'Collective drawing' or a swift guided tour is a good way to negotiate this. Sometimes the drama lesson itself can be very much determined by the definition of space.

For example, a group is in role as 'pyramid designers' [14]. The ageing pharaoh wants an impregnable pyramid designed for this soon-expected demise. They go away in smaller groups and prepare their design. As a whole group, they put together the best ideas to make one design. They build the pyramid, using props or through dramatic conventions (freeze frame, montage). They are summoned to the finishing ceremony, the pharaoh 'conveniently' dies, they are then informed that they, of course, cannot be allowed to leave because they alone know the secret of how to plunder the pyramid - the whole group in role begins as the door shuts, to lock them in.

As pupils become more sophisticated in drama education they themselves become more sophisticated in their use of space, and far more aware of its potential to create good drama. For a final GCSE project a group of fifteen year olds devised a project based around one character. This person was called Kieran, a boy who was deserted by his mother at birth. As he reached adolescence he decided he must set out on a quest to find his mother. He lived in a futuristic land in a small, desolate and icy northern village. He travelled through many places, each carefully defined in terms of space, having numerous adventures along the way, until he eventually reached the big city in the south.

The starting point for the session when he reached the city was to define the space. It was decided that the city was in two halves, a rich and poor sector. We created a divide which represented a wall down the middle. Kieran arrived in the poorer sector, his mother lived in the rich side and was married with a new family of her own. Already the potential for drama was strong. The pupils then decided it was a religious society; they created an ancient statue which was vital to the worship of the religion. This statue was situated in the poor district, the rich wanted to worship without having to cross the barriers and were thus preparing to relocate the statue. A sewage pipe from the rich side surfaced in the poor sector and was polluting the river, their only source of water.

Finally, the poor sector had a great need for cheap and immediate housing, so they were building a block of flats (represented by a scaffolding tower), this was cutting out more and more light to the rich sector. By defining and creating the space, this group had built into the drama considerable tension and possibilities. Careful consideration of situation was largely responsible for the success of this session.

FOCUS, TENSION, SYMBOL AND METAPHOR

Was the focus of and tension in the drama clearly established?

Once you have set up the 'who' and 'where' of the drama, something is still needed for drama to happen; this something is focus and tension. This is not equivalent to open and direct conflict. Once this occurs it is easy for the focus to split and tension to drain away. The creative potential of dramatic tension is located in that period of time immediately before or after conflict has occurred. There is a potential to change a seemingly inevitable outcome and this can be an exciting business. Tension often is generated by knowledge of what has happened prior to the moment of drama being explored. The perspective of past events informs the acting out of present moments.

Take, for example, the proposition of introducing 'Romeo and Juliet' to a group who have no knowledge of the play. The choice of entry into the text is crucial if interest is to be generated. By focusing on one of the many forms of tension Shakespeare employs, a way in to the text can be found. Types of tension have been classified in many ways [15].

Time
We could meet Juliet just after she has spoken to Romeo for the very first time to help her think about the possible consequences of seeing him again.
Responsibility
A meeting with Friar Lawrence after Romeo and Juliet are dead to try to stop him committing suicide because he feels responsible for everything [16].
Mystery
What was the first incident that led the Montagues and Capulets to hate each other?
Secrets
How does Juliet keep her secret from her father?
Ritual
Exchanging insults between the Montagues and Capulets.
Nirvana
If they escape to a different country will all be well?
Dilemma
Juliet loves Romeo but he has killed her cousin who she also loves, what should she do?
Adventure
Romeo climbs over the wall into the enemy's garden
Power/rules
The heads of both families have forbidden contact
Shock/Surprise
Both young people die and everyone else must carry on, the public is outraged. How has this been allowed to happen?
Artefacts
The potion of Friar Lawrence had the power to do great good yet it did great harm.

However we achieve it, our session must have tension. As practitioners we must be aware of this and build it into our session beforehand.

In any drama session, the pupils could follow any strand of the story or issue, and different pupils may well head off in different directions. This can quite easily result in a very difficult situation, or even chaos. It is the practitioner's job to make sure that members of the group are focusing on the same issue and that the focus is on the key point from which the practitioner thinks most learning in terms of content or form may occur.

Without a clear focus, the drama situation can quickly become confused. The most common mistake we make is to try to cover too much ground in a short space of time. Choosing the right focus is about finding the way in to the work which seems to have the most significance and latent potential for learning and enjoyment for the group. Here is a fuller example:

The session was with a mixed ability group of 13/14 year olds. They had requested to do some work on the idea of space. The aim was to present them with a module of work which would challenge their perceptions about the environment. They adopted the roles of Space Cadets on their final day of a seven year training program.

They were set an exercise to devise a method of showing an important visitor that they were capable astronauts. They came up with things like flight simulators to show landing on different planets, emergency procedures etc. The head of the United Nations arrived and they showed their exercises. She (teacher-in-role) watched, congratulated them, presented them with their badges, 'Astronaut-Class 1', and swore them in with their oath of allegiance, which was 'I promise to serve the world and obey orders at all times without question'. They were told that tomorrow they were going on a mission of immeasurable importance, to get a good night's sleep as they were setting out on a three month journey early in the morning. Details of their mission were contained in an envelope with their orders, these had to remain secret for the moment. They were to be opened when they were in the orbit of the planet to which they had been taken. The morning arrived, they boarded the ship and were cryogenically frozen for the duration of the journey.
They awoke to find themselves orbiting a strange planet. As they looked out of the ship's window, they saw a remarkably beautiful planet, green and blue, as Earth must have been at its birth, a whole planet which looked like the Garden of Eden. They assembled to open their orders. They broke the seal and read the orders, 'There is humanoid life on this planet. Locate an alien and bring it back to earth'.

They land the ship and do a preliminary survey of the planet. Teacher in role entered as the alien, an innocent being, harmless and helpless in view of their superior technology. Once basic trust is gained she tells them her story, which includes the following information:

'I am one of only a very few people left on the planet. We are a peaceful race. Thousands of years ago we nearly destroyed our planet through war and pollution. I will have nothing to do with machines, which we banned years ago, I simply believe they are bad. I can ride the wind and have no shelter, as the earth protects me.

I am waiting for the great day. This has been spoken of for generations. Eventually only two of our people will be left, from these will spring a whole new race, this time we will not make the same mistakes.'

The tension for the participants is what to do with this alien. The decision becomes the focus. Do they obey their orders, thus fulfilling their oath, and take her back, or do they leave her there and have to face their superiors when they return? Constant radio inquiries as to their progress serve to reinforce the tension through pressure of time.

Was meaning lacking because symbol and metaphor were not considered?

Alongside tension and focus, symbol and metaphor need consideration. Symbolisation is in some ways the key to learning in drama. The careful selection and introduction of an object can act as a focus for the group's thoughts and feelings. The practitioner can use gesture, verbal and vocal signals to invest an object with meaning and encourage or provoke individual response. A collective meaning may emerge, but the challenge then is to enable each individual to subscribe to or challenge this meaning.

Two objects in this drama were designed as symbols. The first was the badge, symbolic of their achievement, their own pride and the pride of their family and friends in them. Secondly their orders, symbolic of their oath and thus their honour, and their responsibility to others. In a way the alien herself became symbolic, a representative of innocence, hope and future potential. The pupils themselves made the space ship symbolic. It was a machine and represented the force which could destroy the future of a planet. The pupils who wanted to take the alien back felt comfortable in the ship; the ones who did not, left the ship and made a base on the planet's surface.

In a sense the whole drama had now become a metaphor. The decision of what to 'do' with this alien was the decision of what to 'do' with our planet Earth. The alien planet could well be Earth years from now. The alien and her prospective mate could easily be seen as Adam and Eve.

If pupils felt they had to obey orders and take her back because of the cost to them personally if they did not, were they then jeopardising the future of the Earth in the long run because of their inability to make sacrifices themselves? For those who had refused to take the alien back, were they realising just how great a personal loss would be necessary to protect the planet? The issue of what to do with the alien had become a metaphorical discussion of the Earth's environmental issues. If symbolisation and metaphor came out of tension and focus, all were reinforced by the crafting of the lesson, achieved largely through the selection of particular conventions.

CONVENTIONS

Were conventions used dynamically rather than mechanistically?

As discussed earlier, conventions are ways of organising time, space and action to create meaning [17]. They allow all members of the group to participate in the drama in an organised and hopefully challenging way. Different conventions can allow for different levels of participation which often means that at one end of the scale individuals can contribute and participate without feeling that they have to do anything embarrassing. While at the same time other individuals can take on a big personal challenge.

A group experienced in drama will be able to suggest conventions that could be useful to develop the drama. It is important to share these terms with the group from their first drama session. In this way they will be able to make suggestions about form as well as content, and will be improving their drama and theatre skills, knowledge and understanding.

Conventions are not sufficient in themselves to create process drama. It is the transitions and timing, pace and appropriateness of these in relation to the content being considered and feelings and thoughts of the participants that give the drama a dynamic. A string of pre-determined conventions mechanistically worked through will produce a perfunctory piece of work.

The conventions themselves are drawn from a wide range of sources; theatrical, literary, psychological, therapeutic and the arts. Conventions used in one particular way establish a scenario giving clear definitions of role, situation, focus and perspective. They can be used to feed information into the drama and help build the context. They often operate on a narrative or plot level ie what happens next? Used in another way the same conventions can be used to explore areas other than those concerned with narrative, plot development, drama and the art form. They can focus on the symbolic dimensions of the work through careful use of signing and reading. They can give the opportunity for individuals to consider their thoughts, emotions, feelings and understandings in relation to the rest of the individuals in the group. Used in such a way conventions also allow for considered reflection from within the dramatic context.

Games:
played together to focus attention, calm down or wake up, to reinforce, or make concrete, concepts, to reveal the game structure found in situations.

Narrative/voice-over:
commentary/narration: by the leader or a group member over or in front of the action to create atmosphere, give information, help reflection or move the drama on in time, control the action, etc.

Supporting sound/sound tracking:
sounds made using voice/body/musical instruments which are then used to support action. This may be recorded or done live to create atmosphere, consolidate the context, usually used to fit a specific part of the drama.

Drawing together/collective drawing:
the whole group draw on a very large sheet of paper (pieces taped together) or all contribute to it over a period of time, to pool ideas, share perceptions, consolidate the context.

Hot spot/hot seating:
the group interviews a person in role (the groups may also be in role or not) to build characters, clarify perspectives and the context.

Still images, freeze frame, frozen image, tableaux, set in concrete, photo album:
groups or individuals get into a frozen position which may be looked at, and read, by others to focus closely on one moment or to physically express an abstract concept. The images might be presented as part of the drama as, for example, a photo that has been found, a painting, a sculpture, a statue. This is a very versatile convention and can be used as a form of work in its own right.

Interviews/interrogations:
in pairs or groups to give or gain information and build roles. Examples include detectives, scientists, TV researchers, barristers, members of a jury, oral history, etc.

Mind parts:
the group are invited to become various parts of a role or character's mind. The conflict within the mind is deconstructed and the various elements within it identified. The group then choose which element they would like to play. The individual playing the role then stands in the middle of these elements. When she points to an element, that group gives all the reasons why she should act as they wish. As soon as she drops her hand, they must fall silent, even in mid sentence. The role can keep on pointing and listening until she feels a decision can be made. This can be a powerful way to build commitment using teacher in role in the middle of the circle.

Reconstruction/re-run/re-enactment:
the whole group, or small groups. or pairs carefully reconstruct an incident to explore its dynamics and tensions as in real life crime programmes on TV e.g. 'Crimewatch'. Separate re-enactments could be done from different viewpoints.

Hidden thoughts/speech bubbles/thought-tracking:
one person moves and speaks in role whilst the other speaks the subtext, e.g. what the person is really thinking but cannot say. This helps build roles and reveals dynamics and tensions of the situation. Alternatively, one person can be frozen while the rest of the group are asked if they will individually pass behind this character and speak the characters' thoughts at that particular moment.

TV/radio & newspaper report/coverage/media reports:
events are interpreted or approached through the conventions of TV/radio/newspaper headlines etc. This can build context by revealing different perspectives.

Mini productions/teams/small group playmaking/improvisation:
the group splits into small groups to demonstrate alternative understandings which may or may not be shared. This can help build roles and situation and can be combined effectively with teacher in role or used as a means of making a statement about the action as performance.

Parallel story/analogy:
the class works as a whole group or in small groups through parallel situations that mirror themes and dynamics in the agreed area to be explored. This requires and encourages objectivity.

Mantle of the expert/the ones who know:
there are various levels at which this convention can be explored. At its simplest, pupils are endowed with specialist knowledge e.g. designers or historians. When used in full form, specialist knowledge is not endowed but slowly built through carefully identified tasks which require the gathering of more and more knowledge. This task-driven form of drama builds up strong commitment and belief in roles and situation and can become a form of work in itself.

Simulation:
this emphasises the importance of facts and previously identified dynamics rather than creating drama based on individual and group imagination. Useful in providing background to situation, e.g. if a project on unemployment is producing only stereotypical responses to perceived problems, the drama is shelved for a session and an exercise set up in which the weekly allowance is given to family units, plus a list of their bills. What can they afford to eat that week? A list of current prices is provided. Chance cards with additional financial demands are dropped in, e.g. 'It is one of the family's birthday.' The following session, the group returns to the drama with the insights gained from the simulation.

Defining space:
the action is located in a particular space and defined by an agreed method.

Costuming:
can be used to hook interest, generate questioning and build belief particularly when used in a partner-in-role situation. The costume itself may be read in a way which begins to suggest a story about the way a person lives.

Official messages, letters, diaries, journals, documents:
these can allow movement away from the immediate action of the drama and provide opportunities for the consolidation of individual roles. They can also be used to initiate drama as they provide excellent opportunities for thoughtful, well focused problems to be set in context. They can be written in or out of role. Information technology can be very effective, e.g. taped messages or 'last recordings', photographs, video recordings, word processed documents which could, for example, add authenticity to an official letter.

Eavesdropping/Overheard conversations:
the majority of the group listen to a spontaneous or rehearsed conversation between a pair or smaller group. This provides an opportunity to explore different perceptions of the same event. It can add tension as well as feeding information into the drama.

Maps and diagrams:
a collective activity which can be teacher or group led. It can allow the implications of a particular situation to be carefully explored in visual form at the beginning of or during the drama.

Captions/titles:
a phrase/thought/slogan/graffiti is written large on paper and presented with the action of a particular group. The relationship between the physical action and the written work can have its own resonance.

Off-stage pressure:
tension is provided by a force/ power/ person who will soon arrive but is not yet present. This can give impetus to a task which needs completing or a decision which must be made before this arrival.

Partner-in-role:
another teacher/parent/senior pupil provides the focus for the drama. Information is let out very slowly by the role who carefully listens to contributions by the group and responds to signals from the actual teacher. The group are aware of the person playing the role and may well know them, but that person does not come out of role. The teacher uses the dynamic of the space between the group and the role to create tension as implications are carefully explored. The partnership is between the teacher who is controlling the action and the partner who is acting as the live focus.

Role-swap:
at a key moment in the drama, roles are reversed in order to explore the predicament from a totally different perspective.

Forum theatre:
an event/ scene is recreated in detail and then replayed. If anyone feels that they would have acted differently at a specific moment within that scene they put up their hand/shout out. The scene is rewound in order for them to step into the action and try their theoretical idea out in practice. The scene can be fast forwarded/slowed down, new characters can be introduced in order to explore the situation.

Artefacts/unfinished materials:
useful for generating questions to start a piece of drama or to introduce tension during it e.g. a map partially completed, a letter torn, only the opening lines left.

Game shows:
the group agrees to explore a difficult issue through a game show format. For example 'Guess that Prejudice' where a member of the audience who has suffered prejudice is quizzed by the audience who must guess what sort of prejudice they are looking at. The volunteer, who can only answer yes or no, must then recount the incident as quickly as possible to win a prize. The juxtaposition of form and content can be used to start or reflect on a drama.

Teacher-in-role:
a major convention which allows the teacher to challenge, support and develop the drama, and individuals in it, from within the drama. It does not involve the practitioner acting but does require conviction and the adoption of an attitude that can be shown in action. Useful in allowing the teacher to encourage the group to see the possibilities of the 'game' of drama.

Telephone talk/long distance communication /conversations:
two people speak together with the group as audience. To clarify and control the action, introduce new roles, create tension.

Meetings:
where the space is organised in an agreed way and a procedure established for communication to take place. This allows information to be fed in, problems to be debated, roles clarified and built, e.g. a group of protesters, pirates, police, conspirators, concerned members of the public.

Collective role:
often at the start of a drama, participants adopt a 'collective role'. For example, they all become astronauts. The emphasis here is often on establishing the situation, focus and perspective through a general role experience. As the drama progresses, participants are encouraged to make these roles more specific or to adopt others in which they see potential.

Computer input:
an individual, or small group, or the teacher, programmes the computer to give an input to the drama. For example, a communication may suddenly start printing out at a moment in the drama which serves to increase tension and focus activity.

Metamorphosis:
the group or individuals can become inanimate objects. This is useful for defining space and giving detail to location. It allows commentary to be made from a different perspective, e.g. What would be in the old woman's attic when the students entered? In groups of two or three, find a way of representing a specific object they might find.

Either /or:
ask the group to choose between two options which in effect divide the class in half, e.g. 'If you think you would rush and get help, sit on the right of the room. If you think you would attempt a rescue yourself, sit on the left.' This is useful for managing the drama and creating two audiences. Most importantly, it gives the group the opportunity to see that they can determine the direction of the drama. This has to be true, as they all may decide to sit on one side of the room and developments accordingly take place from there.

Continuum:
draw an imaginary line down the centre of the room and place the word 'Yes' at one end of the room and 'No' at the opposite. Place a chair to the side of the room at mid point on the continuum. Ask anyone who wants to, to stand on the chair and ask any question relating to a character or issue that they would like to ask. The rest of the group must then move to yes or no or some point in between on the continuum. This is a useful way to allow individuals to make statements without having to defend them verbally. It allows the group to see physically and visually that there are many differences of opinion in a group.

Moving sculpture/essence machine:
one person is invited to walk into the centre of the room and start repeating a small piece of movement (with repeated words or sounds). One by one, the others join in this moving and audible sculpture. e.g. the title of the sculpture is 'Home'. Individuals in the class could suggest what the subject or name of this might be. This convention can move responses away from the literal to the abstract and conceptual.

Marking the moment/where were you?
each person in the drama is asked to go to the exact place where they felt a significant moment occurred for them in the drama. Some of these can be shared or people can be encouraged to reflect on why this was significant for them. A useful way of reflecting on a session or for gathering thoughts when continuing a drama perhaps a week later.

Role-on-the-wall:
draw around a student on a large sheet of paper and use the outline to represent a character in the drama. Facts or characteristics known or perceived are drawn around or in the shape. It can be useful to contrast the 'outer' impressions with the 'inner' truths which are represented so graphically. Individuals can play this collectively agreed-upon figure.

Montage:
selected images, sounds and movements are juxtaposed to evoke feelings and thoughts generated in a drama. Useful in consolidating work or reflecting upon it.

Masks:
can provide a protected way in to drama. The making of these allows discussion to take place prior to the action and reduces possible perceived threats. Also a distancing device.

Puppets:
again a safe way in to drama work which allows time for discussion during the making process. Also a distancing device.

Mime:
individuals or small groups communicate with the rest of the group using their body rather than words. This can encourage participation for those who feel unsure of speaking.

Empty chair:

place a chair in the centre of a circle. Agree upon and then envisage a chosen character sitting in it. The group asks questions of him/her. The group answers its own questions through the chair, being sensitive to the logic and consistency of the replies.

Two groups - two people:

split the group. One person faces the other whilst the rest of the class stand in two groups (one group behind each individual). The two groups must whisper what they want their individual to say to the other individual. The individual is a mouthpiece for one group. This allows a large group to shape a conversation between two people.

Echo:

the physical setting is the same as 'Two groups - two people', but in this convention the group is the mouthpiece of the individual and can only act as an echo. Useful in building up tension in a conversation between two people which actually involves a whole group. To add tension, the individuals and the groups can physically move towards each other during the conversation. The two individuals at the front of each group lead the speeches which must be in short phrases or sentences to work.

Song:

taped or sung live, this can be used to complement or provide a contrast to action or to reflect on or in a drama,

Sculpture:

one person models an image by physically manipulating an individual or group of individuals. Useful in exploring individual perceptions and can be developed by subsequently exploring 'ideal' images and the realistic possibilities of transition between them and those first created. Much of the value of this convention lies in the rest of the group reading the image, i.e. saying what information and/or feeling this gives them.

Tunnel of decision/conscience corridor/conscience alley:

the group form two parallel lines and try to verbally influence the decision of the individual who walks down the alley between them. By the time the individual reaches the end of the alley/corridor, she or he must have decided on a course of action in response to arguments/chants/pleas. Useful in consolidating individuals' decisions, thoughts and feelings.

Dance past:

two people are asked to represent the protagonists in a pivotal moment in the drama. The group is then asked if, individually, they would like to take it in turn to model that volunteer into a physical position which they feel literally or abstractly represents their emotional state. When a number of modellings have taken place, the two volunteers are asked to remember the four positions which really captured how this character was feeling.

The group is then split in two and half goes with one volunteer, half with the other. The volunteer then repeats the four physical positionings and then runs them together with link movements to form a short dance/movement phrase. All of the half-groups then learn this phrase and practise moving it across the room. When both groups are ready, they stand at opposite sides of the room and rehearse by simply walking the way they will move past each other to get to the opposite side of the room.

After the rehearsal, music and lighting can be added as the two emotions dance past each other. Just before they do this, they are asked to reflect on the feelings and emotions they experience as they dance past the others.

Ceremonial action/rituals & ceremonies:
to show or create a set of repeatable actions, gestures, visual statements that are part of a specific culture or are particular to one person or group of people. They may be devised to honour specific events or may be observable parts of life. These may be rituals of an opening ceremony.

In the Space Mission pretext described on page 18, a context-building convention was used to define space within the space ship, sleeping berths, where the windows were and a central area where the crew could meet to open the orders.

Another narrative-based convention was used on the eve of the astronauts departure. They had an imaginary phone call with the person dearest to them to impart the news of their departure and to gain the person's reaction to their absence. They then developed this by being put on to different people such as a parent, brother or sister, or a friend. Another convention was the frequent radio contact with earth. Tension was increased by putting more pressure upon them, for instance by saying that they had to return to earth sooner, or that some military support was on its way.

A reflective and evaluative convention which could be used is role reversal. After two distinct groups had formed with opposite views about what to do with the alien, dialogue between the two ceased. To allow them to see both sides of the issue more clearly we swapped attitudes briefly, so that the group who wanted to bring the alien back had to take on the attitude of wanting to stay with him on the planet and vice-versa.

Finally another reflective and evaluative convention was used at one point when the alien was positioned in the middle of the room and everyone was asked to stand in relation to him matching how they felt about him to their chosen physical position. Close to him if they felt good about him, far away if not. This was developed by adopting a stance to further illustrate feelings. For instance one person standing well away from the alien turned his back, another made as if to strangle him.

QUALITY OF INTERVENTION

Did you intervene effectively?

No matter how you have planned a session, or in whatever direction or style it is developing, there will always be times when the group takes the drama on in their own way, especially when working in whole group in role.

In the 'Crash Landing' pretext (page 78) the group are placed in the archetypal situation of a group of people who suddenly find, as a result of a disaster, that they have to survive in conditions very different from those they are used to. When the group are clear about situation and role, they will want to start exploring and living on the island. If you are in role with the group you will be joining in this activity, or you may choose not to be in role and sit out and observe the drama. If you are sitting outside the drama then you have withdrawn, your decision about when to get involved again is also the decision about when to intervene.

If you have set up a situation so that you can withdraw, for example, once the survivors wake up on the beach, then the decision that faces you next is when to intervene. As leaders we need to watch and listen very carefully to what is happening. Only through careful attention to what is going on can we make the right decision. In one lesson I was disturbed in this observation by a colleague who distracted me on 'urgent' business. By the time I could again pay attention to the drama, I had lost the threads of the work which were important to individuals in the group. I could find no way to intervene constructively, apart from stopping the drama and asking them what they felt had become important.

In the end, I allowed them to carry on for the whole session. This can be the worst kind of leader withdrawal. I do not know how many opportunities were missed. Individuals were not really involved in drama, they were playing. Withdrawal can, of course, be absolutely necessary for all sorts of reasons. Time is often needed to develop the work, be it development of role, space, belief or simply on a narrative level.

It is easy for a leader to fall into the trap of taking over and dominating the session, for example, building the shelter. You cannot do that if you have withdrawn. The other advantage of withdrawal is that it gives you the potential of re-entry for a positive intervention at a later point which might be more useful.

In the session when I did not intervene, there was no focus, small groups were involved in lots of separate activities, I needed to intervene to provide the focus. I could have entered as a traveller, someone who knew the area and could warn them of the floods that would come next week etc. Whenever a leader intervenes it should be thought out carefully. Will they accept an intervention at the point you have chosen? An unsuccessful intervention can destroy the drama, it will at least be met with blank, bemused faces before they carry on doing exactly what they were doing before!

An intervention does not have to be done in role. It is often valuable to stop the drama and seek clarification. You should know what is going on, and it will clarify the situation for the rest of the group, who may be engrossed in one activity at the expense of the whole group focus. Clarification can of course be done in role and this is often more valuable. Clarification of people's feelings, beliefs, attitudes and values often goes hand in hand with clarification at a narrative level.

Pace is often a vital consideration for intervention. A variety of pace within a session is important. If a meeting has become bogged down, for instance, intervention to move the drama on may be needed. If the group are rushing headlong into the final conflict it may be necessary to slow the action down, use a reflective convention to encourage more thought about the issue, slow the pace down and use strategies to deepen the work.

A drama pretext has **a pivotal point**. This can be crafted, as for example in the World War One role play when the German officer enters, (page 13-14) or it can just happen. You need to recognise this and intervene appropriately to offer the possibility of deepening understanding.

'Working on your feet' i.e. spontaneously, is at the heart of a drama practitioner's work, and perhaps the most difficult part of the process to analyse. The success of intervention and withdrawal depends on so many variables and teacher judgements, there is no formula that can guarantee success. Each piece of work will have its own rhythm, its own dynamic, and this needs to be felt by the leader. At times it will feel right to switch to a contrasting activity or physical grouping . For example in 'Dirty Clothes' (page 38) with one group it may be important to keep switching the whole group between the world of animals and that of humans. With another group it may feel right to let roles develop steadily in two distinct sub-groups. At other times the deliberate juxtaposition of style used may re-capture the group's interest or re-focus them. For example, if interests dwindles early in the narrative of 'Dirty Clothes' it might be appropriate to inject a modern parallel true story about child neglect, or facts from the NSPCC to illuminate the analogy. In other instances it might feel right to persevere with one strategy or convention. On the simplest level, when interest is draining away it may be time to negotiate a change of strategy or convention. On another level, you may feel that a group is working well but that the level of challenge in the work needs raising through a change in form. The clue seems to be in developing a sensitivity and 'awareness of need'.

This involves developing an awareness of when to withdraw and when to intervene. It involves experimenting with variations on the two, with different paces and rhythms in order to generate possible learning moments.

As it is difficult to read a group simply by visual observation, it is important to seek verbal clarification from individuals to check their perceptions of the work.

QUESTIONING

Was your questioning effective ?

A vital part of any drama lesson is questioning. This takes place on different levels before, during and after the drama.

Before the drama it is important to consider the closed information-generating questions you will be asked when building the context. It is also vital to pinpoint the key 'organising' and 'open' questions to which you, as a leader do not know the answer, but which you are interested in exploring with the group.

During the drama asking the 'right' question at the 'right' time to the 'right' individual/group, in the 'right' way is a skill that can be developed. This can increase the level of challenge for the committed or, equally, regain the interest and re-focus the attention of the uninterested. You also need to consider the most effective way of asking certain questions at certain points would be in or out of role. Closed questions can be very powerful in role.

After the session, appropriate questioning can obviously allow the group to reflect upon the drama skills, knowledge and understanding generated. It has been said that 'the two worst forms of knowledge are ignorance and certainty'. The aim of process drama work is to find the 'right' questions to ask, rather than fixing upon immediate answers and solutions.

When working on types of questions, we find the following classification to be useful [18]: Examples are given from 'Dirty Clothes' (page 38).

What?

itemises, lists, gives opportunities for non-threatening participation, invites speculation, eg 'What sort of animals would you find in the forests of North America?'

Where? Who? When?

generate specific information and build context, eg 'Where is the rest of the village? Where are the forests?'

Could? Would?

explore potential and offer opportunities for participation eg 'Could we just practise it?...Would someone draw on this map..?'

Will? Can? Have?

demand commitment eg 'Have you ever met anyone like this hunter?'

How?

considers feelings eg 'How do you think she felt at that moment? How can we move the drama forwards?'

Drama can be used to exercise our feelings of sympathy and empathy. Too much emphasis on asking members of the group 'how' they feel can be as counter-productive as not asking them to consider the inter-play between their role or beliefs and that of the character or attitude that they are portraying.

Why?

asks for explanations. Most of our questioning is designed to find out 'why?', yet this question can be the least useful if asked too prematurely. Explanation needs to be teased out by using other kinds of questions. The 'why' is often the overall drive of the lesson and should be worked for. If you know the 'why' the drama is often all over. e.g. 'I wonder why nothing seems to have changed in the hundreds of years that have passed since the time of Dirty Clothes? Why don't people intervene if they know someone is being abused?'

Much of the purpose for asking questions in drama is to fulfil the needs of **reflection, analysis and evaluation.** Reflection upon dramatic work is crucial if participants are to have an understanding of the work. But reflection need not take the form of discussion immediately after the drama. Reflection can be productive and significant when articulated within the context of the drama or outside it, during or after the process is complete.

EXTERNAL FACTORS

Did external factors affect the session?

Because process drama often works by gradually and carefully building an agreed imagined context, participants need the opportunity to concentrate on the immediate construction of this. External factors can intrude into the building of this 'other world', and destroy a session, particularly with groups that have a poor social health or who are not used to this method of working.

Physical interruptions into the space can be disastrous. Forty minutes can be spent constructing a context, slowly building the possibilities for belief and moving to the pivotal point of a drama, only for a phone to ring or a member of staff, the secretary, or someone to come in with a message. On some occasion when interruptions are frequent this can mean that to all intents and purposes the session can never move beyond the superficial. People can perhaps be forgiven for interrupting process drama as to the uninformed eye it often looks as though nothing very much is going on. Lines are not often being 'declaimed', the atmosphere is often relaxed and there is laughter. The fact that thirty people have carefully negotiated and constructed a fictional context within that space is not always obvious to those who enter part way through this process.

One way around this is to inform people about 'how' they can enter during sessions, people often understand if you explain yourself. One teacher, because of a pastoral role he was performing in the school found some interruptions were unavoidable. He struck up a deal with people who were likely to enter, they came in through the side door, sat as an audience and would wait until he could withdraw, thus reducing the interruption greatly. This also is a useful strategy for members of the group who arrive late.

An example is due. The project was a four week module with a mixed ability group of 11/12 year olds, looking at a cross-curricular project, drama and technology. Planning was meticulous. We studied 'Technology in the National Curriculum' and isolated four broad areas which we felt were especially pertinent to drama; these were listed under the devised headings and we give one level as an example of each.

Other Cultures
Know that in the past and in other cultures people have used design and technology to solve familiar problems in different ways.

Describing and Working with Others
Recognise the points of view of others and consider what it is like to be in another person's situation.

Changing Needs
Review the ways in which their design has developed during the activity, and appraise results in relation to intentions.

Designing and Making
Use talk, pictures, drawings, models, to develop or design proposals, give simple reasons why they have chosen to make their design.

Very briefly, the context was established, using 'mantle of the expert'. Members of the group were in role as the members of various design firms who were tendering for the contract of designing the first city on the moon. Design was interlaced with in-role work when the group were the first people to live in the city, their experiences were then to feed back into the design proposals.

Session 1 was good, then came the externals! During Session 2 I had to moderate GCSE work, the lesson was covered by a supply teacher in an English classroom and the work I set was not attempted. I taught session 3 and arranged for the head of Technology to come in and give them some skills input on design. I got a phone call at lunch time to say that his moderator had turned up and he could not make our lesson. The pupils arrived, very late, hot, flustered, and with glazed over eyes. I was told that two pupils would be even later as they had been sent to the Head of Year Seven for fighting in the street on their way to drama. I effectively talked to myself until the two 'heroes' arrived. We moved to the art room and I tried to give the skills input. I left the art room last and arrived at the studio to witness a flying drop kick. The victim bursts into tears and I had words with the aspirant 'Bruce Lee' who then also burst into tears. I gave up on the drama lesson and the class went home. External factors had taken over.

Mood is a significant factor. Your own mood as a teacher is important. To launch process drama well you need to be on top form. This is not possible all the time, nor is it desirable to sustain such a high level of input and energy week after week. If you are not up to it don't try it, you can end up doing more harm than good. Move into exercise or small group improvisation or rehearsal mode. Pupils' mood also comes into play i.e. the mood of a whole group, not just an individual, though we have to cope with individual's moods for the good of the whole. Events prior to individuals entering the drama space bear directly on it. An experienced practitioner will read the class and individuals in it well and angle the drama to suit the mood.

Possibly the most important factor outside the drama itself is social health. Many of the real difficulties in teaching process drama stem from social ill health [19]. There is no short cut when trying to improve the way a group of individuals relate to each other. Drama can allow individuals to experiment with other behaviours but they are unlikely to do this unless there is a measure of trust between themselves and with the practitioner. In some cases a total lack of trust makes it impossible to do drama with a group. There are strategies to try in such situations, many simply to do with good teaching, but such changes take a long time. For example, focus strongly on negotiating and adhering to the drama contract established. Make the social health of the group an explicit issue in positive terms. When the contract is broken, consistency is needed in applying agreed sanctions.

Individuals in the group need to be treated with unconditional positive regard at all times [20]. This does not mean that frustration cannot be shown. Alternative ways into the work for individuals that cause particular problems could be considered. This could be through technology, perhaps using the video camera, audio taping, computer or lighting. Other professionals or interested people could be invited into the sessions. The value of such a 'third dynamic' in settings where groups have poor social health cannot be over-estimated [21].

If just one individual or a small group is continually disruptive, it can be difficult, if not impossible, to do any drama. Often the rest of the class ends up disciplining the person who is 'spoiling their drama', who has in effect broken the contract which allows drama to work. We have seen many cases where drama has allowed individuals who are normally disruptive to succeed and become motivated through this success. For example one of the most frequent feedback comments on the drama we get from prisoners we have worked with is 'It's kept us out of trouble for three days' (or however long the project is). On the other hand, we have experienced cases where just one individual can sabotage a motivated and keen group and where exclusion has been the only answer. 'This group was great before.......arrived'. One person can ruin a theatre performance for the hundreds of people in the auditorium. The same is true in drama education. The difference is that perhaps there is room for much negotiation before the play finally stops.

Many groups who have poor social health can find ways of working together through drama, albeit inconsistently. However, sometimes it does not matter what you as a teacher do or have prepared. External factors can be too problematic for drama to happen. In such cases it is best to 'let go' and have a fall-back position planned. This may be to finish a session after ten minutes good work rather than plough on with a further forty minutes chaos. If this is not possible the teaching style may have to change. For example a more didactic whole group approach could be used or group or individual tasks introduced.

In the short term we may often fail in our aims and objectives because of factors beyond our control. An individual or group cannot be 'forced' to imagine, play, pretend or act. As drama practitioners we must recognise this, be stoical, forgiving of ourselves, and come back to the struggle renewed for the next session.

A CHECKLIST FOR REFLECTING ON A DRAMA SESSION

Summary Sheet

Had the CONTRACT been established to mutual satisfaction?

If no   Do you need to re-negotiate the contract for the session?
           Are there ways in which the group's ownership in terms of content and form could be increased?
           Does your long term contract need re-negotiating?

Were the LEARNING OUTCOMES for the participants clearly understood?

If no   Could you identify outcomes that are drama specific/social skill based/knowledge or content based and agree these with the group?
           Are outcomes inappropriate and do they need re-negotiating?
           Were the group aware of their responsibilities or could these be clarified?

Were your AIMS appropriate?

If no   Would it be useful to identify a specific target for work with this group?
           Would it be useful to identify specific targets for certain individuals?
           Did you as practitioner really want to explore something in this drama?
           Were you committed to the stimulus?
           Can you clarify what it is that intrigues you in this material
           in terms of form and/or content? (If you are not interested it is
           unlikely that the group will be).

Were the participants ROLES clear and developed and was your role (if used) effective?

If no   Was the status of roles appropriate?
           For example, were they too close to actual life roles? Could alternative roles that are closer or further from the participants actual status be introduced?
           Were the roles age appropriate and were participants protected in to these?
           Were the participants given the chance to adopt, sustain, develop and interact in role?

Was the stance of your role effective? Were the signals given by your voice, posture gesture etc. read in the way you had planned? Was the role you took on too close to your own persona to be effective? Could you change role? (It is hard to change the register of an existing role once established). Could partnership in role have added to the session, if used was it effective? Could prepared roles have added to the session, if used were they effective?

Was the SITUATION clear, appropriate and effective?

If no   Was tension considered and built e.g. was it clear to the participants what had happened in narrative terms prior to the moment they entered the drama? Was the task itself clear and interesting?

Did you create an appropriate atmosphere e.g. did you use lighting and if so was this effective?

Would the creation of an environment have helped, if you did was it an appropriate and effective environment?

Was the physical space organised and clean? Was the imaginative space clearly defined in all the participants minds?

Were resources used to their full potential and had research been done to inform the context?

Did participants respond appropriately to created atmosphere and try to add to it?

Was there a clear FOCUS and TENSION within the drama?

If no   Did the initial frame hook interest?

Was there enough tension to get commitment?

Could you identify possible tension(s) that could have been injected?

Was 'the game of drama' operating i.e. the ironic, fun side of the work?

Was the perspective (the events leading up to the moment of entry in to the drama) clearly established?

Was meaning lacking because symbol/metaphor were absent? What could have become symbolic/invested with meaning to give depth?

Were CONVENTIONS used dynamically to create an aesthetic rather than mechanistically to control?

If no   Did the use of conventions generate clear, achievable, interesting yet challenging tasks for the participants? Did the conventions used build belief?

Was the pace too slow or too fast?

Were group sizes varied for tasks ?

Did you make demands intellectually, physically, emotionally, spiritually as the drama developed?

Which conventions worked and which were not effective? Which other conventions could have been used instead?

Are you using the same conventions and strategies in a predictable pattern in every drama you do? Could you experiment and take risks with other conventions you feel less secure of?

Could you ask the group which convention they would like to use at a particular moment to give choices?

Was your QUALITY of INTERVENTION effective? Were you effective in identifying and responding spontaneously to ideas and feelings?

If no   Did you withdraw from the work at the right moments?

How useful were your interventions?

Did you intervene to clarify the drama, was this successful?

Did you need to give more clarification at any point?

Was the pace of the session right (too fast/too slow)?

Was there enough variety of pace?

Was there a planned pivotal point in the session? Was it reached? Did you use it to good effect?

Did you pace yourself in the course of this session? How involved were you in the course of the session and within the overall scheme of work for this group. e.g. were you working too hard for too long or the reverse?

Did you set the appropriate tone for the work e.g. demanding authenticity and commitment at one point whilst encouraging laughter and distance at another?

Did the participants display an ability to work independently when you withdrew?

Was your QUESTIONING technique effective?

If no   Did you use closed questions or use them to good effect in role?

Did you ask helpful context building supplementary questions?

Did you really want to know the answer to some key questions?

Did you question in role?

Did you ask questions of individuals rather than to the whole group?

Did you make time to quietly talk to, and question individuals whilst the rest of the group were working?

Was your method of questioning skillful overall? i.e. did it support, confirm, challenge, allow time for reflection?

Did you build in time for reflection and analysis within the drama?

Did you build in time for evaluation at the close of the session?

Was there a need for the group to be de-roled and/or de-briefed?

Were EXTERNAL FACTORS a problem in this session?

If yes   Were interruptions a problem? How can they be avoided in the future?

What was the mood of the participants like when they entered the room? How did you take account of this?

If the group, or individuals in it, have poor social health did you try to balance short term and long term goals and did this work?

Does your analysis of the social health of the group suggest that ways need to be found to move forward in terms of behaviour management and motivation?

INTRODUCTION TO THE PRETEXTS

These pretexts can be used with all ages and abilities. We realise this is quite a claim, but we stick by it. They have developed from initial ideas through years of trial and error into their present form. You will, of course, change and develop them, improving them into texts that work for you.

Aims and Learning Outcomes given for each pretext are examples only. You, or your group, may use the pretext for different purposes and the aims and learning outcomes would naturally change. We have not specified cross-curricular links in all cases, as they are embedded within all of the pretexts.

Each pretext is printed in two forms. Firstly, as a narrative which outlines the drama in detail (instructions in the narrative are in italics). Secondly the pretext is given in grid form for quick reference or to reflect upon and deconstruct a session. This highlights the reasons behind steps taken and suggests where a particular emphasis should be given to sustain the drama.

Timings for activities have been left largely to the discretion of practitioners. You will know your group best and may well need to be flexible anyway. A short amount of time can, on one occasion, focus thoughts and ensure quality work, whilst on others it produces only a superficial response. Similarly, a longer time span can, on one occasion, lead to lack of purpose and direction whilst, on another, can allow in-depth, thoughtful, quality work to emerge. When our experience in running the pretext tells us an activity usually does benefit from a particular time limit, we have broken the rule and presumed to give one.

The over-all amount of time spent working with a group on a pretext is also left up to the individual practitioner. We have used pretexts occasionally as one-off sessions but usually employ them as a basis and an essential structure for a full half term's work or project. As has often been said, in drama education quality work comes not from having dozens of bright ideas, but rather from one good idea, carefully developed.

Dirty Clothes

Based on a story from North America told by Hugh Lupton
Used with upper primary, secondary, 16+, undergraduates, PGCE, in-service & community

Aim
To provide a safe framework for the exploration of the sensitive topic of cruelty to children and bystander apathy.

Learning Outcomes		
Drama Skills	**Social Skills**	**Learning areas**
Adopt, sustain and develop two contrasting roles	Empathy	Cruelty to children and human rights
Control of movement and voice to suggest a quality rather than literal representation	Respect for other cultures and views of reality	North American Indian traditions
Demonstrate an awareness of focus and tension	Respect for animals	Assertiveness

Resources
Large paper, felt pens, crayons, an item of clothing that symbolizes 'Dirty Clothes'. A short Native American Indian call and response (3 repeated calls and 3 echoed responses) needs to be sung at the start of work in the contract session and repeated at a particular point later in the drama.

Contract
This drama will involve you playing many kinds of roles from humans to animals. It is set in North America where the native Indian people are renowned for their knowledge and respect for all animal life forms.

Song
At one point in the drama it would help if you could sing this very simple response to these words. Could we just practise it: "Haaiieea, Haaiieea, Haaiieea." *(This is sung in a North American Indian style, soft and lamenting.)*

Narration
A girl once lived with her uncle in a rough cabin on the edge of a village where life was hard. Behind the hut the trees ran up and up to the bare rock of the high mountain tops. The uncle treated the girl very badly.

Role on the Wall

These are the two main characters in our drama.
Draw outline figures for the uncle and the girl. Tape each to the back of a chair and label one 'uncle' and one 'girl'.
As our story drama develops we will find information about both of them and we can 'flesh-out' these outlines. This might be useful as some of you might play these roles. To start with I will play them so you get an idea of what they are like.

Narration

The uncle used to make his money by selling the skins and flesh of the animals he hunted in the huge forests to the people of the village. He was the best hunter and the people were afraid of him. But they needed the animal meat, furs and skins to survive. No one dared to speak against him. They were worried about the girl who, after the last snows and her mother's death, had come to stay in his cabin.

List Making

What sort of animals would you find in the forests of North America?
Make a list.
We will come back to these later.

Map Making

If this is the uncle's cabin that I'm drawing here where is the rest of the village? Where are the forests? Could someone draw these on the map please? Does anyone else want to add any more details?

Role on the Wall

Have we found anything out yet about the girl or her uncle?
Fill in details in the outline figures.

Narration

The people in the village were right to worry about the way the girl was treated. Her uncle never spoke to her except to tell her to stay near the cabin. He would rise with the sun, untie his dog from the tree outside and disappear into the forests until dusk fell. Then he would return, light the fire, skin the animals he had killed and roast some meat. The only food the girl got was scraps thrown from his table. The only warmth she got was from the embers when her uncle had fallen asleep and she could creep closer to the dying fire. The only clothes she had were some cast-off animal skins that were so tattered they were not fit to sell. These clothes earned her the name in the village of 'Dirty Clothes'.

One day her uncle arose and said to himself: "This girl is a thorn in my side with her miserable looks. I will be rid of her." So saying, he called her to him and told her that she would be accompanying him that day. She didn't know what to say but blindly followed him out in to the early morning light. He walked straight past his dog and into the forests.

Soon they were climbing higher and higher up out of the forests on to the bare rock. Her thirst was great by the time the sun was fully above but she dared not complain. Then he stopped in front of a dark, gaping cave and spoke. "You go in and flush the animals out. I will kill them as they run out," and he strung an arrow on his bow. She was scared but had no choice.

She moved into the darkness and felt her way along the cave wall. Sharp corners stuck into her, webs brushed across her face but she went on. She reached a dead end and her head turned towards the entrance. There were no animals. As she looked down the long passage a huge boulder was rolled over the entrance to the cave and the little circle of light was blacked out completely. She ran and stumbled her way to the entrance, grazing and cutting herself on the way. The rock was massive. She pushed against it but it did not move. Then all the fear and misery came rushing out of her and she fell to the floor and cried. She remembered her mother and a song she had taught her when she was a child and she sang it there in the darkness.

Song: I will be Dirty Clothes and sing heiieea, heiieea, heiieea you be the echo and respond to me. Great. Can we try that again and make it even more mournful.

And out of the darkness came the voices of her ancestors

Song: "Heiieea, heiieea, heiieea". Response: "Heiieea, Heiieea, Heiieea."

The huge great rock was rolled back and Dirty Clothes stumbled out in to the sunlight blinking in the brightness. There was the most amazing sight. All around her was a circle of all the animals of the forest. The deer were there, the wolves, the bears the.......etc.

And the ....spoke *(choose a strong group)* and said "Come and live with us because" ....and the ....spoke and said "Come and live with us because" ....and........and Dirty Clothes didn't know what to say or who to choose but she knew she need never live with her uncle again.

Small Group Work

Get into groups of 4/5 and decide upon the type of animal you want to be. For example, you could all be wolves, all bears, all eagles. Whatever you choose, everyone in your group should be the same type of animal- you live together. Let's hear what groups of animals we have and I will mark where they were sat in this circle around Dirty Clothes.

This is the task; work out what you would say to Dirty Clothes. How would you persuade her to stay with you so you could claim that honour? Use all the characteristics and knowledge of the animal you have chosen to try and persuade her.

Teacher in Role & Small Groups in Role

I will play Dirty Clothes. Try and persuade me as I talk to each group in turn.

Narration & Teacher Selection of Strongest Argument

In the story the arguments were just as strong as yours but she had to make a choice and Dirty Clothes chose to go and live with the......bears. *(Or any other animal you choose as long as the rest of the narrative can be manipulated to accommodate this creature).*

Narration

Let us leave Dirty Clothes there for a minute. Her uncle made his way back down to the cabin. People from the village watched him come back. They had heard his dog howling all day long, they knew something was wrong. They had not seen Dirty Clothes outside the cabin at all. When he returned earlier than usual with no animals they began to talk to each other.

Pair/Group Work

What do you think they were saying? Remember they don't know what he has done. Maybe someone saw him leave with Dirty Clothes, maybe not. Certainly no one followed them as he would have heard them as he as such an expert hunter. In pairs or groups begin a conversation which shows your response. You have just seen him walk back in to the cabin.

Narration

Even though the villagers had their suspicions, none of them dared say anything. But when he came in to the village to sell some furs that he had in store they tried, very carefully, to find out what was going on.

Teacher in Role

As the hunter I will come up to you as a villager. Try speaking to me in role and see if you can find anything out.
You want some of these skins?........What do you mean asking me about this and that? She has gone to see her family over the mountains etc.

Hot Seat

Teacher in role as the uncle portrayed as a violent uncompromising man who only has respect for the the 'survival of the fittest'. Questions from the group to be asked out of role.

Role on the Wall

Can we add anything else to the character of the uncle? I'll write them on here with the earlier comments. What about Dirty Clothes? Do we want to add anything else? Let's go back to her now.

Narration

She could not have had a better time. During the day she rolled around and played with the young bears and at night the older bears looked after her and protected her as one of their own. In the long summer months she also began to change. Every time one of the young bears scratched her as they played a most amazing thing happened - hair grew in its place. Very soon she had been scratched so many times that she had a coat of fur just like the rest of the bears. A long winter of snows passed. Spring came and then the first of the long summer days. She was so happy.

One day they were all lolling around when there was a cracking of wood far in the distance. The bears froze. It was a hunter. Then there was a sneeze and they all relaxed. "Its only 'Old Coughing Lungs'," they laughed., "He won't worry us," and they slowly ambled off to safer grounds.

The next day again as they relaxed came another sound of a snapping branch. They froze. Then there was a bump and a moan. "Don't worry, it's only 'Old Clumsy Feet', he's probably tripped up again," and they laughed and ambled off to safer grounds. The next day came another snap of a branch and again they froze. They heard the sound of sniffing and leaves and silence. "Quick, run!" they shouted. "It's 'Two Legs-Four Legs' the most dangerous hunter of the forests. Run now if you want to live." They ran up and up the mountain side until the trees began to thin out and the bare rock began to appear. Two Legs-Four Legs was catching up fast. They all climbed up inside a huge old hollow tree, one on top of another, stacked high and still. Then the sound of sniffing. Silence. Then came the sound of twigs being gathered. Then the striking of flint and the smell of smoke. He had lit a fire at the bottom of the hollow tree and was smoking them out.

Down they came, tumbling on top of each other their eyes watering. Dirty Clothes rubbed her eyes again, blinking because of the light and the smoke. There in front of her, with an arrow about to be loosed into the largest bear of them all, was her uncle – Two Legs - and Four Legs of the dog. Now she understood. She cried out, "No!"

As she spoke all the hairs fell from her body and she stood once again in the dirty clothes she always wore. Her uncle stepped back in amazement, but he didn't drop the bow. He kept it pointing at the bear. "You, follow me or the bear dies," he said. Dirty Clothes had no choice. If she said no he would surely shoot the bear. She hung her head and silently made her way down the mountainside. As her uncle led the way into his cabin Dirty Clothes felt that she was the unhappiest person on earth.

She didn't see the boy of her own age watching from the edge of the village. As soon as they had gone in, he ran back with the news. Dirty Clothes had returned.

Either/Or

Ask the class which of their two roles they would like to work on next, the human or animal. Ask them to move into one of these two groups. Then, as that group in role, start the action from [A] Animals: the moment after Dirty Clothes and her uncle disappear from their sight. [B] Humans: from the moment the boy runs in to the village with the news that Dirty Clothes has returned.

Branch Planning

Defining space/ forum:

Define the space of the uncle's cabin in detail. Two volunteers, or teacher in role. One volunteer to improvise an incident that happens on the first night Dirty Clothes spends in the cabin. The scene can be replayed according to forum practice until the whole group feel they have found some ways forward for Dirty Clothes.

Group Sculptures

Ask the group whose thoughts and emotions they would like to consider at this moment in the drama. They have four choices: Dirty Clothes, the uncle, the animals, the villagers. The task is to create a group sculpture that expresses the thoughts, feelings and emotions of the character(s) or group chosen. Give time for preparation. Each group in turn watches the others and 'reads' their sculpture for meaning.

Discussion & Small Group Play Solutions

Broaden the discussion about Dirty Clothes' plight to that of other children who are treated cruelly. NSPCC information could be introduced. What should we do if it happens to us or we feel this is happening to someone we know? A solution in connection with Dirty Clothes or based on a parallel situation is rehearsed and presented to try to show the difficulties in dealing with such situations.

Dirty Clothes

	Step	Reason	Convention	Emphasis
1	Explain that the drama involves taking on the role of humans and animals.	To give the drama credibility by referring to a cultural context where animals have as much significance in adult as in children's lives.	Contract.	In North Western America the Native Indian people are renowned for their knowledge and respect for all animal life forms.
2	Sing a call and response North Western Native American Indian song.	Gain initial involvement. Set up this call and response for use later in the drama.	Song.	Stress that the ability to sing well is not needed in this song.
3	Tell the first lines of a story.	To hook interest.	Narration.	The girl was treated very badly.
4	Draw an outline of two characters and tape on the back of two chairs.	Let the group know that they can help build characters.	Role on the Wall.	Stress that this could be useful later when members of the group take on these roles.
5	Tell the story up to the point where the girl has gone to live with her uncle.	To establish the power the hunter has physically and economically over the rest of the people.	Narration.	The people needed the hunter's furs and food to survive.
6	Ask what sort of animals you would find many years ago in the forests of North America.	To disentangle the past of the drama from the present and introduce possible roles to be used later.	List Making.	This tale happened many years ago.
7	Draw the uncle's cabin which is separate from the rest of the village.	To define the landscape of action of the drama.	Map Making.	Refer again to the past. A time, for example, before roads reached into the mountains.
8	Ask if any more details have been learnt about the two central characters.	To continue character building.	Role on the Wall.	Encourage their 'reading' of character.
9	Tell the story until the uncle returns to his cabin.	To set up a piece of pair or group work in a clear and developing context.	Narration / Song.	To establish the cruelty of the hunter and his powers.
10	Ask the group to split into 4/5s and choose to be one type of animal grouping eg. 5 bears, 5 wolves, 5 eagles. How would you persuade Dirty Clothes to stay with you?	To increase the level of participation and provide contrast with the previous activities.	Small Group Task.	Really use the act of persuasion and use your imagination in this task. There can be many and varied viewpoints in responses, but they all were afraid of him.
11	I will play Dirty Clothes. Try to persuade me.	To project people into animal roles through an enjoyable but challenging task.	Teacher in Role. Small Groups in Role.	Talk to one group at a time. Encourage ironic responses and level of game in the drama. They had their suspicions but none dared say anything openly.

Dirty Clothes continued

	Step	Reason	Convention	Emphasis
12	Choose one of the groups to go and live with.	To ensure that everyone feels their input has been valued.	Selection and Narration.	Emphasise that she will live with each group for one year each before moving into storytelling.
13	Describe the scene where the Hunter returns without Dirty Clothes.	In pairs or groups take on the roles of people from the village and improvise the gossip about this.	Narration. Pair or Group Work.	The nature of this gossip can vary from speculation to indifference. All the villagers are afraid of the hunter, they also rely on the food and furs he provides in the winter.
14	Set up the scene where, as teacher in role, you try and sell furs to the villagers.	To provide another set of perspectives on the situation. To establish the hunter's power and hold over this community.	Narration, Teacher in Role, overheard conversation.	Emphasise the fear and dependency the villagers feel and suggest that any questions about Dirty Clothes will have to be circumspect.
15	Teacher in role as the uncle, portrayed as a violent, uncompromising man, who only has respect for the 'survival of the fittest'.	To show how difficult it is to challenge such a powerful figure face to face.	Hot Seating.	The uncle has a completely different set of values. He respects animals for their strength of purpose and hates humans for their gossip, chatter and weakness.
16	What do we know about the character of the hunter? Recap and speculation.	To establish that this character has a very different view of the world from most people but that such people do exist.	Role on the Wall.	Ask if there is anything about the hunter that can be admired.
17	Rejoin the story of Dirty Clothes and her first year with the animals and tell until the point when she is seen returning to the cabin after a whole year has passed.	To switch focus again in the drama and examine the situation from a different perspective.	Storytelling.	Use the animal that Dirty Clothes chose to live with earlier in the drama. Emphasise that a full year has passed.
18	Ask individuals which of the two roles they would like to work with, animals or humans.	To allow individuals to begin to assume responsibility for the direction of the drama in terms of form and content.	Either/or.	It does not matter if everyone wants to continue with animal roles or everyone with 'the humans'.
19	Discuss form and content. How do we develop the drama from here?	To give the group responsibility for developing the direction of the drama according to their wants, needs and purposes.	Discussion.	Clarify possible issues within the drama to look at eg. domestic violence.

King Lear

Based on Shakespeare's 'King Lear'
Used with primary, secondary, 16+, undergraduates, PGCE, in-service & community

Aim

To introduce the text of King Lear and identify possible areas of interest to the group and individuals within it.

Learning Outcomes		
Drama Skills	**Social Skills**	**Learning areas**
Creating costume	Team work	Power of words
Writing a monologue	Co-operation	Love
Manipulation of tension	Utilising others' ideas	Truth

Resources

A bundle of newspapers, T.V., video player, camcorder, video tape, tape recorder & player for music whilst making. Felt tips x 24, large paper for role on walls, text extracts, videos of different versions of the play e.g. Lawrence Olivier, Michael Hordern, Paul Schofield.

Contract

This pretext is based on selected parts of Act 1 Scene 1 of Shakespeare's King Lear. You do not need to know anything about Shakespeare's play but I hope this work will make you want to read or see it. If you do know the play that is fine and you may want to re-visit it after the work. We are going to create our own version and, if you want, we could watch different versions of Shakespeare's opening scene performed by professional companies on the video to see how they compare to ours. We will use his plot and some of his language when it might be helpful.

We will start by acting out the first scene of the play and then taking it from there, but first we will make costumes for the characters.

Making/costuming/paper technology

We are going to make everything out of newspaper and it should look very good, very professional, let me show you. (See diagram 1). Just watch this, get one of these pieces of paper, lay it on the table or floor like me and fold the corner over. Then roll it slowly ...so you make a paper rod. See how the ends are floppy but the middle is really strong. Just the smallest piece of masking tape will hold it as a rod. Could you hold this while I rip a piece to put on.

I pass my paper rod to someone who looks as though they might just help me. They are obliquely brought in to the drama by helping me out. This is the whole aim of the paper technology exercise - to give a chance for those who are initially hostile to join in without losing face. For whatever reason, the activity of paper technology has its own rhythm and momentum. Once people start to create with it they begin to talk and cannot help but touch each other as they pass materials, comment and laugh at their results. This is also a very non-threatening approach to work. People are being given time to consider characters and the dramatic situation before grappling with Shakespeare's language, which can be daunting for groups with no experience of it. It is in this sense that the participants are 'protected into' the drama. Contrast this with, for example, the use of theatre or drama games as a starting point. These require participants to interact with one another immediately. A making activity allows time to elapse and talk to be exchanged before this decision has to be made. The more carefully the trust is built up in the first stages of the drama process the more likely it is that risks will be taken later on in the drama. This is a key concept in the work.

Choose the individual who you feel has shown the most involvement to date.

Would you mind being a model for the costume you are going to create? You don't have to 'do' anything

Begin to build a head dress (see diagram). Keep reassuring them that it will look good but they have got to give you a chance. Be encouraged by any comment no matter how damning. Upgrade everything that is thrown at you e.g. "It looks like a space monster." Which could be echoed back as: "Well Shakespeare was writing in the late 1500s, early 1600s but there is nothing to stop us setting it in the future. Many directors have done just this". Really the 'game of drama' is beginning to be played. The group may be trying you out, to see if you do listen or are there to tell only. Respect usually comes when it is clear that you do take every idea as a genuine one.

Discussion of images/Role taking/prepared roles

When the head-dress is complete, model it in a coloured light. This could be simply an OHP covered with lighting gel or from a small rig bought in for the drama. The 'professionalism' lies in the image cast in shadow on the wall behind the head-dress/costume (see the example, page 59). Point to the shadows of the hat and begin to tell about the character of either Cordelia or Goneril, depending on what the hat suggests e.g. open/ naive/ honest or cunning / subtle/ vulgar.
Make a chair available for the character to sit on and write out her name for the others to see. Stick it to the back of the chair. Pull out another four chairs.

We are only going to work on five characters

Write out the names of Cordelia/ Goneril / Regan/ Kent/ King Lear and ask them to listen to your brief outline of their character before they choose which costume they would like to work on.

Cordelia, a central character, is the youngest daughter of a king. She loves him more than her two older sisters ever could and he loves her more than anyone. She is, however, very honest and open. In a court that almost entirely is made up of flatterers, she is regarded by them as naive. But she is honest, with an intense stubbornness. Her costume should show this.

Goneril, a central character, is the eldest daughter of a king. She can flatter and win-over anyone. She has no shame in the lies she is prepared to tell to get what she wants. She is cunning, subtle, vulgar and ruthless, but can hide all this at an instant. She believes her youngest sister is a fool but knows her father loves her best. She believes she can pull the wool over her middle sister's eyes anytime.

Regan is the middle of the three daughters in terms of age. She, like Goneril, is cunning, subtle and very good at flattery. She believes she can persuade her father and her two sisters to do what she wants.

King Lear's costume will have to fit me, as I would like to play him in the opening scene. He is old and takes himself very seriously. He has had enough of running the kingdom and wants to retire and have an easier life. He is, however, a very bad judge of character and loves listening to flattery. He intends to hand over his kingdom, in three parts, to his daughters but typically asks for something that a more humble person would not. He asks each of his daughters to step forward in front of the whole court and say how much they love him. He is vain, arrogant and stubborn.

Kent is the closest friend of the King. He knows Lear is making a mistake in handing over his kingdom to his daughters. He loves his friend very much and, as he has known him such a long time, speaks to him more like a friend than a subject, which could be seen as quite dangerous in those times. He is honest, kind, compassionate and strong.

Choose which character costume you would like to work on. The costume must be durable. It must be able to stand being worn off and on for performances over the next few weeks. I will come round and answer any questions you may have about the characters - what we know and what we don't know.

Out of role discussion and information feeding

As you move around the groups and/or help individuals work on the costumes, feed in information on the characters and ask questions in ways that give ideas for the costumes e.g.

King Lear has power of life and death over everyone at the start of the play, what could we make to show this?

The activity does not have to be rushed. The relaxed atmosphere of making, or just watching the making, is an essential part of gaining commitment for the drama.

Costume presentation/Mime/Model

When the costumes and props are ready, get each group to present their work. Put light on it and re-cap the characteristics of that role whilst pointing to the shadow of the costume and interpreting what it might suggest or signify. Suitable music can be added if desired.

Storytelling

Now we have the roles, let me tell you the outline of the opening of the play and then we could do some work on it and then act it out.
The play takes place in a kingdom where the old king had ruled for many years and kept the peace.

In the re-enactment, the group look at the map the Lear group has drawn.

The king decided that it was time to rest, that the responsibilities had weighed heavy for too long, he would divide the kingdom up in to three giving his youngest and favourite daughter the most opulent part.

In the re-enactment, divide the map in to three, with the richest part clearly identified.

He called his daughters together and asked each to step forward. The eldest, Goneril, flattered him incredibly saying that she owed him everything and that the very sun shone from his eyes along with many more compliments.

The next, Regan flattered him even more to the point where she said life had no meaning without him. The youngest, and one who loved him most, Cordelia, stepped forward and said nothing. She could not bear what she had heard and was not going to play the flattering game just to please him. She knew she had always loved and cared for him and that her sisters did not care at all for anyone but themselves. She could not "heave her heart in to her mouth" as she says and so says nothing. The King's disbelief turns to anger. He warns her to think again and asks how someone so young can be so cruel. She replies that she is so young but so true, and that he can not see true worth even in his own family. When the youngest had refused to flatter a second time (despite the warning that "nothing shall become of nothing"), he banishes her.

Small Group work

In the groups that have made the costumes devise/write lines/speech for your character to help that person in your group deliver it. Have some fun with the outrageous nature of the hollow compliments. Here are some parts of the scene from Shakespeare's play that you can use or adapt or just look at (Page 54). The group that have helped make the Lear costume, could you make the huge map of the kingdom whilst the others are working on what they are going to say?

Go around and help the groups.

Define space/Re enactment/Teacher in role

We are going to re-enact the scene as discussed. Can we agree on where Lear enters from, where do the daughters stand/sit when giving their 'testimonies'? Should the rest of us watch in role as members of the court or simply watch as audience? While you are watching or participating in the scene I would like you to be thinking about what scene should follow this one. I will tell you who Shakespeare focused on but in this pretext you can decide.

We will list all the options open to us.

Get decisions on these points and then re-enact the scene heightening the language and interweaving play text as appropriate. Either the teacher or a member of the group can play Lear, both have advantages and disadvantages. Choose whichever allows the group to feel that they have achieved a creditable performance in a short space of time.

Video

The scene could be videoed and watched and/or Act 1 Scene 1 of a film version of the play could be watched and used as a comparison. The level of interest in usually high. Comments such as "... that's not as creepy as our speech" ... "she's good"...or "you're a better blagger (liar) than she is...you should hear her with" ...etc.

Question to select focus/Ownership

Who should we look at now in the drama? What scene would you like to make and look at?

Choose a response and create the scene. Clarify the frame i.e. roles, situation, focus and perspective. This is the point where the group's agenda can perhaps be identified. What is it in the play as presented up to this point that has a resonance in their experience, or their lives?

For example, when we ran this pretext with a group of women prisoners they were interested primarily in the power battle between the two elder sisters. That was the scene they chose to reconstruct the next time we met. I was cast in the role of a formerly powerful lord. Whilst the two of them met to talk about who had control of me I had to scrub the floor. This is something the women have to do every morning on their hands and knees with a scrubbing brush and polish. As they feigned aristocratic accents, arguing over who had control over me, one of them waited till I had 'cleaned' a sizable area, someone else sitting at the side shouted out "Walk all over his clean floor"... "Slowly" added someone else. We re-wound the scene and they took enormous pleasure in letting me clean and then ruining the work. This had happened many times to them.

In the following week, they chose to focus on Cordelia, who, they said, would have been locked up in the dungeons with rats. They built a prison cell and made more keys. The task was to get her out. The attempt failed and she died. The strongest sister ruled the kingdom.

*In terms of plot this concluded a four week, one day a week, project. We videoed the work as it progressed. Each day started and finished with a viewing of the video of their work. On the final day of the fourth week the women invited the officers in to watch their play of 'King Lear'. It was theirs in the sense that they chose the aspects of the play that interested them and engaged with the issues relevant to their situation.**

Branch Planning

- A meeting between the two sisters or Kent in forum

- A split group conversation between Kent and Cordelia.

- Hot seat Cordelia.

- Conscience alley - Does Cordelia risk going to speak to her father? Does Lear go to speak to her? - Does she really disappear from his mind?

- Role on the wall - each major character

- Split into groups: Conflict and possibilities of peaceful resolution in families.

- Edmund & Edgar figures.

- Nature/Nurture. Look at the scene Shakespeare wrote next i.e. Act 1 Scene 2. This could be read or watched first on video.

King Lear

	Step	Reason	Convention	Emphasis
1	The pretext is based on selected parts of Act 1, Sc. 1 of Shakespeare's 'King Lear'. We are going to perform our own version of this.	To acknowledge and anticipate fears or misconceptions about Shakespeare's work.	Contract.	You do not have to know anything about Shakespeare's play. Hopefully you will want to know more when we start work on it. This is our interpretation. We can use Shakespeare's language as and when we find it useful.
2	Demonstrate paper technology basics and ask the group to help you 'mass-produce' the sorts of materials that will allow professional costumes to be created.	To protect participants into the drama. Focus is taken away initially from Shakespeare's language and placed on a concrete, achievable activity.	Making/Costuming/ Paper technology. (See page 00)	Upgrade comments made and discuss how professional companies have used many sorts of materials in production to great effect. Ask the group to bear with you and 'professional costumes' will be created.
3	When you have completed one demonstration head-dress, use an OHP or other light source to look at the shadow it creates. Introduce key characters.	To demonstrate how professional the costume's shadow can look. To begin the introduction of key characters.	Shadow projection. Production.	Coloured gel, a simple light source can give impressive results. Point to the characteristics of the person suggested by the costume.
4	Tape the names of Cordelia/Goneril/ Regan/Lear/Kent on the back of five chairs and ask for small groups to costume one person according to the information given on them.	Begins to move from costume to character.	Out of role discussion. Small group work.	Give a time limit for costume making eg. 20/30 minutes, but if it is going well let it run. Put music on, let the activity be relaxed so you can feed character information in as necessary.
5	Rehearse how the character is to move and enter the space. Give a choice of music.	A move towards performance and representation.	Small group work. Costume presentation.	Praise and upgrade all contributions.
6	Narrate the opening of the play until Lear arrives.	To define the context.	Storytelling/ Narration.	Listen to what your characters do and the way they interact with each other.
7	Devise/write lines for your character which will form the basis of the script in our version.	To offer Shakespeare's language but only as needed by the groups.	Small group work. Costume presentation.	Praise and upgrade all contributions.

King Lear continued

	Step	Reason	Convention	Emphasis
8	Perform the scene as outlined. Teacher (or member of the group) in role as Lear.	Give a sense of achievement. A performance quickly realised.	Define space re-enactment. Teacher in role.	Rehearse briefly positioning. Give role to rest of the group as members of the court invited to watch Lear hand over power. What scene would you like to see next? Video performance. What did Shakespeare look at next?
9	Watch this performance on video and other televised/videoed versions of this scene.	To allow comparisons of approaches and see how different interpretations result in different productions and designs.	Video.	Encourage comparisons of 'effectiveness' according to interpretation.
10	What scene would you choose to write/devise next? Which do you think Shakespeare did?	To identify the subtext in the play that this group would like to explore.	Discussion/Questions to select focus.	List options of next scene, see who would like to look at what. Describe or watch Shakespeare's Act 1 Sc. 1.

An extract from King Lear, Act 1 Scene 1

Characters

LEAR	King of Britain
GONERIL	Lear's eldest daughter
Duke of ALBANY	her husband
REGAN	Lear's second daughter
Duke of CORNWALL	her husband
CORDELIA	Lear's youngest daughter
Earl of KENT	Lear's adviser and friend
SERVANTS	

There is a fanfare. A servant comes in carrying a crown. Next, King Lear enters followed by the Dukes of Albany and Cornwall with Goneril, Regan. and their attendants.

Lear: Meantime we will express our darker purposes.
The map there. Know we have divided
In three our kingdom, and 'tis our first intent
To shake all cares and business off our state,
Confirming them on younger years.
Tell me, my daughters,
Which of you shall we say doth love us most,
That we our largest bounty may extend
Where merit doth most challenge it?
Goneril, our eldest born, speak first.

Goneril: Sir, I do love you more than words can wield the matter;
Dearer than eyesight, space, or liberty;
Beyond what can be valued, rich or rare;
No less than life; with grace, health, beauty, honour;
As much as child e'er loved, or father, friend;
A love that makes breath poor and speech unable.
Beyond all manner of so much I love you.

Cordelia: *(aside)* What shall Cordelia do? Love and be silent.

Lear: *(to Goneril)* Of all these bounds even from this line to this,
With shady forests and wide skirted meads,
We make thee lady. To thine and Albany's issue
Be this perpetual.—What says our second daughter?
Our dearest Regan, wife to Cornwall, speak.

Regan: Sir, I am made
Of the self-same mettle that my sister is,
And prize me at her worth. In my true heart
I find she names my very deed of love—
Only she came short, that I profess
Myself an enemy to all other joys
Which the most precious square of sense possesses,
And find I am alone felicitate
In your dear highness' love.

Cordelia: *(aside)* Then poor Cordelia—
             And yet not so, since I am sure my love's
             More richer than my tongue.

Lear: *(To Regan)* To thee and thine hereditary ever
             Remain this ample third of our fair kingdom,
             No less in space, validity, and pleasure
             Than that confirmed on Goneril. *(To Cordelia)*
             But now our joy,
             Although the last, not least in our dear love:
             What can you say to win a third more opulent
             Than your sisters?

Cordelia: Nothing, my lord.

Lear: How? Nothing can come of nothing. Speak again.

Cordelia: Unhappy that I am, I cannot heave
             My heart into my mouth. I love your majesty
             According to my bond, nor more nor less.

Lear: Go to, go to, mend your speech a little
             Lest it may mar your fortunes.

Cordelia: Good my lord,
             You have begot me, bred me, loved me.
             I return those duties back as are right fit—
             Obey you, love you, and most honour you.
             Why have my sisters husbands if they say
             They love you all? Haply when I shall wed
             That lord whose hand must take my plight shall carry
             Half my love with him, half my care and duty.
             Sure, I shall never marry like my sisters,
             To love my father all.

Lear: But goes this with thy heart?

Cordelia: Ay, good my lord.

Lear: So young and so untender?

Cordelia: So young, my lord, and true.

Lear: Well, let it be so. Thy truth then be thy dower;
             For by the sacred radiance of the sun,
             The mysteries of Hecate and the night,
             By all the operation of the orbs
             From whom we do exist and cease to be,
             Here I disclaim all my paternal care,
             Propinquity, and property of blood,
             And as a stranger to my heart and me
             Hold thee from this for ever.

Kent: Good my liege—

Lear: Peace, Kent. Come not between the dragon and his wrath.
          I loved her most, and thought to set my rest
          On her kind nursery. *(To Cordelia)*
          Hence, and avoid my sight!—
          So be my grave my peace as here I give
          Her father's heart from her.
          Cornwall and Albany,
          With my two daughters' dowers digest this third.
          Let pride, which she calls plainness, marry her.
          I do invest you jointly in my power,
          Pre-eminence, and all the large effects
          That troop with majesty. Ourself by monthly course,
          With reservation of an hundred knights
          By you to be sustained, shall our abode
          Make with you by due turns. Only we still retain
          The name and all the additions to a king.
          The sway, revenue, execution of the rest,
          Belovèd sons, be yours; which to confirm,
          This crownet part betwixt you.

Kent: Royal Lear,
          Whom I have ever honoured as my king,
          Loved as my father, as my master followed,
          As my great patron thought on in my prayers—

Lear: The bow is bent and drawn; make from the shaft.

Kent: Let it fall rather, though the fork invade
          The region of my heart. Be Kent unmannerly
          When Lear is mad. What wilt thou do, old man?
          Think'st thou that duty shall have dread to speak
          When power to flattery bows? To plainness honour's bound
          When majesty stoops to folly. Reverse thy doom,
          And in thy best consideration check
          This hideous rashness. Answer my life my judgement,
          Thy youngest daughter does not love thee least,
          Nor are those empty-hearted whose low sound
          Reverbs no hollowness.

Lear: Kent, on thy life, no more!

Kent: My life I never held but as a pawn
          To wage against thy enemies, nor fear to lose it,
          Thy safety being the motive.

Lear:	Out of my sight!

Kent:	See better, Lear, and let me still remain
	The true blank of thine eye.

Lear:	Now, by Apollo—

Kent:	Now, by Apollo, King, thou swear'st thy gods in vain.

Lear:	*(making to strike him)* Vassal, recreant!

Kent:	Do, kill thy physician,
	And the fee bestow upon the foul disease.
	Revoke thy doom, or whilst I can vent clamour
	From my throat I'll tell thee thou dost evil.

Lear:	Hear me; on thy allegiance hear me!
	Since thou hast sought to make us break our vow,
	Which we durst never yet, and with strayed pride
	To come between our sentence and our power,
	Which nor our nature nor our place can bear,
	Our potency made good take thy reward:
	Four days we do allot thee for provision
	To shield thee from dis-eases of the world,
	And on the fifth to turn thy hated back
	Upon our kingdom. If on the next day following
	Thy banished trunk be found in our dominions,
	The moment is thy death. Away! By Jupiter,
	This shall not be revoked.

Kent:	Why, fare thee well, King; since thus thou wilt appear,
	Friendship lives hence, and banishment is here.
	(To Cordelia) The gods to their protection take thee, maid,
	That rightly thinks, and hast most justly said.
	(To Goneril and Regan)
	And your large speeches may your deeds approve,
	That good effects may spring from words of love.
	Thus Kent, O princes, bids you all adieu;
	He'll shape his old course in a country new.
	(He leaves)

NEWSPAPER COSTUMES

TAKE A SHEET OF NEWSPAPER AND FOLD → AND AGAIN → AND AGAIN → UNTIL YOU CAN ROLL IT TIGHTLY → INTO A ROD !!

FIX WITH A SMALL PIECE OF TAPE

RODS CAN BE FLATTENED AND CURLED

PLEAT A SHEET OF PAPER

FIX AT ONE END WITH TAPE TO MAKE A FAN

TAPE AT THE CENTRE

JOIN THE TWO ENDS TO MAKE A ROSETTE

TWIST PAPER

MAKE A ROPE
USE TO WIND ROUND AND TO DECORATE

MAKE A BASIC HEAD PIECE

USE THREE FLATTENED RODS

JOIN WITH TAPE

PLEAT FROM CORNER TO CORNER TO CREATE A POINTED FAN

USE FANS, RODS AND TWISTS TO DECORATE HEAD PIECES AND BODY PIECES

EXAMPLES OF
NEWSPAPER COSTUMES

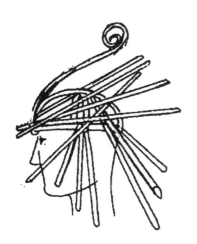

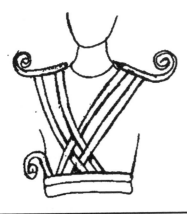

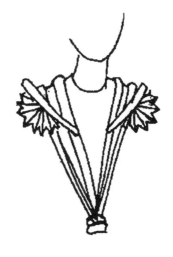

Miranda Zupp

Used with primary, secondary, undergraduates, PGCE, in-service, community.

Aim
To mobilise the energies of the class quickly and get a fragmented group to work together.

Learning Outcomes		
Drama Skills	**Social Skills**	**Learning areas**
Re-enactment with particular attention paid to tension, climax and resolution	Working together quickly in a whole and small groups	Gender and its representation in films
Costuming as a reflection of character	Developing other people's ideas	Stereotyping and the effects of this
Manipulation of character, plot and story	Verbal presentation of ideas	Science fiction as a genre
The contribution of technology to drama		

Resources
Lighting - OHP with coloured gel, lots of newspaper, masking tape. Optional: suitable music for a crowded bar scene and 'the presentation of the Glenturian guards'.

Storytelling

I'd like you to listen to this story.

The shuttle pulled into the space port. Gracefully she manoeuvred the air lock, and there she stood. Miranda Zupp, inter-galactic mercenary. Tall, beautiful, terrifying. She had been summoned to pick up her next mission, and must choose her team from the elite of the Glenturian guard. "Weaklings", she thought.

She hadn't had a proper drink for seven months, and she was about to put that right. The nearest bar looked like a dive, but it would have to do. "Gimme a whisky, and leave the bottle." She downed two glasses straight off, then turned slowly to survey the bar. The usual motley crew of space-travellers, ship hands and space vagrants.

One man returned her stare. He was part of a group of Zeluvians. Eight feet tall, blond and well built. Too long in the bar, too much to drink, he was about to make the biggest mistake of his life. Pushing aside a chair he sauntered up to Miranda Zupp. "Hello darling, how about a kiss for a lonely space traveller?" She stared right at him, he missed the venom in her eyes. He reached over roughly and grabbed her shoulder. In a flash the two fingers of her right hand sank into his eyes - a warning. He lurched back, pain written all over his face. Then the expression changed from pain to anger, then from anger to uncontrollable fury. He went for his weapon. Twenty seconds later seven Zeluvians lay dead, a ripped out throat twitched on the floor. Miranda had only needed her bare hands.

She finished a third glass, paid the stunned landlord, and headed for the door. She needed a long sleep. Tomorrow she would get details of the mission, and she had a very funny feeling about this one, a very funny feeling indeed.

Re-enactment

Let's recreate this story as a piece of theatre. Has anyone seen 'Return of the Jedi' the second of the original Star Wars films, when they go into the bar and it is full of all different types of aliens?

Allow time to discuss and share ideas.

Well let's try to recreate the story as a piece of theatre in the style of Star Wars and a classic Cowboy-Western scenario. i.e. a hero, but in this case a heroine, enters a bar full of villains. The worst villains decide to pick on this 'stranger in town' but their confidence is misplaced. The stranger turns the tables on them and coolly leaves the scene.

Define Space

Where shall we put the actual bar? Do we want someone serving behind the bar?
Who wants to go and build the bar? Will you help?
Will there be any waiters? (Who would like to do that?)
Where will the Zeluvians sit? How many shall we have? Who wants to be a Zeluvian?

Choose Miranda based on your knowledge of the group.

Miranda, would you go and wait over there?

We all need to be in this scene as the motley crew. Everyone go in and get where you think you should be.

Does anyone want to be the band?

Give the group a few minutes to find their space and start to think about their role.

Right - let's do the scene up to where Miranda enters - we'll use the stage lights. Start as soon as they come on. You are building up the atmosphere of a busy intergalactic space bar.

Re-enactment

Let the scene run.

Evaluate

How did that go? Do we need to do anything differently? When do we want Miranda to enter?
What reaction does her entrance get?
How about if everyone freezes and stares at her?
Let the scene run
Did that work? You didn't seem to stop what you were doing. If she is tall, beautiful and terrifying wouldn't her entry be a big thing?
Let's try it again.

Re-enactment

Well done - now - what is the script - pick it out from the story. Can we differentiate between stage directions and what is actually spoken.

"Gimme a whisky and leave the bottle"

She downs two glasses straight off, then turns slowly to survey the bar.
The Zeluvian returns her stare. He is drunk. He pushes aside a chair and saunters up to her.
"Hello darling, how about a kiss for a lonely space traveller".

She stares. He misinterprets. He grabs her. She sinks her fingers into his eyes. He pulls away in agony. His friends get up to join him. He goes for his weapon.
The bartender sinks down behind the bar. Everyone else gets under the tables. The lights go out. The Zeluvians then make noises in the dark as if they are being beaten up and lie as though flung on the floor or against the walls. The lights come up again. They are all dead on the floor - one flexes his fingers like a twitching throat.

The reaction from the rest of the space bar. Miranda slaps her hands (as if to say,'that's that, job over'), finishes her drink and leaves.

Re-enact it until the group are satisfied with the finished product. Music could be added to contribute to the atmosphere being built.

Discussion

So where does the drama go next?
Follow the group's suggestion - or steer it towards where she gets her mission. Who gives her the mission and what is it? (e.g. to renounce violence and find her former self, to rescue the stolen diamond...etc).

Forum Drama

Let's look at the scene where she gets the mission. Who would like to be Miranda this time? Who wants to be the Emperor? Would anyone else be there? How would the room be organised? Who would stand where?

Narration

Now Miranda has got the mission. She has to choose from the elite of the Glenturian guard.

Costuming

I want you to split into groups of 4-6. When I say, "Now" - I want you all to collect some newspaper and a roll of masking tape. I want each group to make the costume of one of the people she chooses. Now there are several ways you can use the newspaper

(See pages 58-59 for suggestions and pages 46-48 of the King Lear pretext for how to explain paper technology)

Make your character very interesting and possessing special/unusual/useful skills. One of you is to model the costume and freeze as the character - the rest must present the character in whatever way you want. We need to know all about them - name - age - talents etc. "Now".

Present the characters, use appropriate music to allow the group time to watch the costumes moving in the space and discuss.

Branch Planning

From this point on the drama needs to go in the direction the participants take it.

Examples :

1)   Forum theatre of the journey to 'find herself'.
2)   The capture and interrogation of Miranda whilst on her mission.

Miranda Zupp

	Step	Reason	Convention	Emphasis
1	Tell the story.	Engage initial interest.	Narration.	Tell it in an 'over the top' way so that they know they are supposed to have fun.
2	Reproduce the story as a piece of theatre.	Develop the character of Miranda.	Re-enactment / Discussion / Evaluation.	Make it into a piece of theatre with which they are pleased.
3	Through negotiation with the group, organise the setting of the scene.	To establish points of entry and areas of action in the scene clearly in the participants minds.	Defining space.	Take a strong lead in organising the space but give enough time to clearly establish the space in the participants' minds.
4	Let the scene run. Rehearse how the character is to move and enter the space. Give a choice of music.	To give a sense of achievement through staging the scene in such a short period of time.	Re-enactment.	Consider where the focus would be in this scene and how we might e-work moments to create the necessary tension after we have run it though this once.
5	Get feedback from the group on what they felt worked, what did not and what could be given attention.	To develop the understanding of dramatic form.	Evaluation.	Try suggestions out.
6	Re-enact the scene again.	To work on dramatic form until the group feel a sense of achievement.	Re-enactment.	Stop the scene if necessary eg. if focus and tension need attention to 'make the scene work'.
7	Early the next morning, Miranda has to choose between the Glenturian guards. In groups of 4/6 make a costume for the guard. This should embody all the qualities you think would make her choose your guard rather than another groups.	To give the group more responsibility for developing the work.	Discussion/Forum drama.	To increase the sense of ownership. With the group, devise the scene where Miranda gets her mission.
8	Re-tell the scene where Miranda gets her mission.	Let's develop the other character she takes with her. Establish further characters.	Costuming.	Make sure you have bin bags ready to clear the newspaper at the end of the session.

The Four Sectors

Used with upper primary, secondary, undergraduates, community.

Aim

To develop pupils' negotiation-within-the-drama skills.

Learning Outcomes		
Drama Skills	**Social Skills**	**Learning areas**
Map Making	Negotiation	International Relations
Defining Space	Creating an Environment to Live in	Contracts
Ceremony	Ritual	Use of Power

Resources
Large paper, marking pens.

Narration

Ask the group to come and sit around you.

I'm going to start by reading a short passage.

In the future there are far too many people on the planet Earth. It must get rid of some of its population. So whole groups of people go to live on other planets throughout the galaxy. One recent settlement was made up of four distinct sectors. The planet itself did not have an oxygen environment, so a grand dome covered the four sectors. There was a central area with a machine which produced the oxygen. The machine was controlled directly from Earth. Communications were received from the satellite computer.

Split the participants into four groups.

Small Group Improvisation / Narration

In your groups perform a small group play which contains all of the following scenes:

1. Show what the world is like in the future - it could be overcrowded, polluted, and impossible to find either a job or anywhere decent to live.
2. A TV advert which advertises life on a new dome-type planet.
3. A discussion of your friends/family where you decide to go to live on the new planet.
4. The journey to the planet.

Show and discuss the plays.

Recap - read the narration again.
Clarify that they are a group who has decided to go and live on one of these sectors.

Map Making / Presentation

Out of role - give each group a sheet of large paper with a 'sectioned circular corner' marked in - for the dome - which they must leave blank, and some felt tips.(See diagram below)

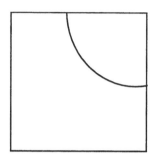

Each group now has a piece of paper which represents their sector. Put together, they form the ground area of the dome.

On your piece of paper design your sector. Bear in mind things like physical geography, housing, leisure, energy, transport, food and water, waste, etc. You can make your sector into the type of place you want. This is your chance to build your perfect world.

When they are finished ask each group to hold up their designs and explain them to the rest of the groups. Try to get everyone in the group to contribute verbally. At the end put the four pieces of paper together to form the complete dome. This will reinforce their uniqueness as a sector, but reaffirm their unity as a whole dome.

TV Advert

Imagine your sector is built, and that you are now living in it. Unfortunately you still need a few more people from Earth to make it complete. Devise a 30 second TV advert that would make people want to come and live in your sector.

Discuss with them successful TV adverts and the possible techniques they could use. e.g. humour, interviews, song, dance etc.
Show and discuss.

Small Group Improvisation

Imagine you have now lived in your sector for several years. Perform a small group improvisation which shows what everyday life in your sector is like. Nothing major is to happen - yet! - we are looking at the organisation/patterns of normal everyday life. You may want to include a scene which shows how you make decisions as a sector.

Ceremony / Ritual

Imagine you have now lived in your sector for many years. Would you devise and perform a ceremony/ritual that is part of your new society. Traditional ceremonies we have today include things like weddings, funerals, special days, etc. Remember, yours is a completely new society, your ceremony/ritual could be about anything you want and may well be very different from the ones we have today.

You may want to discuss what drama techniques are useful in ceremony/rituals. e.g. music, movement, speeches, responses etc.
Show and discuss. Compare and contrast the sectors.

Define the Space

Can we now define the space of this room so that we can work in our own sectors? Leave a space in the middle for the oxygen machine. That could also act as an area where we could meet if we ever wanted to discuss things as a whole dome.

Whole Group in Role

Can we now try the whole group in role, just let the play develop, everyday life in your sector. In a while I am going to enter in role as a representative from Earth. Feel free to respond to my entrance. Right, get into a freeze position ready to start the play. When I clap my hands, start the play."

Count to 10 to get them into a freeze position. Clap your hands. Let the play run.

Teacher in Role

Teacher in role enters the central area. Go into each sector in turn and mime carrying out a geological survey of the rocks beneath the sector. When you have done this ask for a meeting in the central area with representatives from all sectors.

Meeting / Whole Group in Role

Meet with the representatives. The rest of the group watch out of role. You need to get the following over to them.

Thank you for meeting with me. My name is Mr. Williams, Head of Resource Allocation - Earth's Central Committee. I hope everything here is going well? As you know Earth is still a little overcrowded, but things are much better now. Our main problem remains the disposal of nuclear waste from the nuclear age in the 20th and 21st centuries. No more waste can be stored on Earth. Intergalactic law prevents it from being sent out into space. This means we need to dispose of it on our satellite planets. Your dome has been allocated 50 barrels of waste. These will be buried deep under the surface of the dome. They cannot of course be buried in the middle sector because oxygen is produced from there. Thus they must go into one of the four sectors. This is not negotiable - remember it is Earth that directly controls the production of your oxygen! All of the four sections have proved suitable for waste burial. Any land outside the dome is not suitable - far too unpredictable. You must decide which sector is to be used - it cannot be split among the four because of cost. It is expensive enough to dig one hole. I will return in about a week to receive the details of your decision. I can take a few brief questions.

You may need to reiterate much of the above information through questioning.

Branch Planning

Whole Group

Let the play run. It can go off in any direction. One strategy is to change your role to a member of one of the sectors. Arrange a secret meeting with another sector and draw up a treaty - we will not vote to have it in your sector if you vote not to have it in ours. If together you can do a deal with another sector, then you may well have a solution! If, however you have isolated a sector with a particularly strong character in it then you may well not have a solution! This can soon develop into a replica of international relations - meetings, plots, plans, bargaining, treaties, alliances and then counter plots and counter alliances.

Evaluation

Wherever the drama goes it is important to evaluate issues raised along the way. For example; Should they have stuck together and defied Earth? Was their decision fair? Was there an abuse of power etc.?

The Four Sectors

	Step	Reason	Convention	Emphasis
1	Set the scene.	Give a lot of information in a short space of time.	Narration.	These are just the bare bones for the group to flesh out.
2	Show what Earth was like.	Reinforce the need to leave.	Small group improvisation.	The four parts of the play.
3	Design your sector.	Create their own world.	Map making / Presentation.	It should be a world you would really like to live in.
4	Perform a 30 second TV advert.	Reinforce the investment in the new world.	TV advert.	Can be fun.
5	Show what everyday life is like in your sector.	Develop place and roles.	Small group improvisation.	Normal everyday life is all we want.
6	Devise a ceremony/ritual to make a rite of passage.	Start to examine any philosophical/spiritual aspect of the new community.	Ceremony / Ritual.	Try to show how different your society is.
7	Divide the room into sections.	Boundaries will be crucial for the future conflict.	Define the space.	Leave a space in the middle for a meeting area.
8	Let the play run.	Explore role within the new situation.	Whole group in role.	Please respond to my entrance.
9	Enter as Earth representative.	Inject tension.	Teacher in role.	Be low-key, smile, non-threatening.
10	Spell out their problem.	OK. Take the play where you will. To clarify the dramatic situation. To shift the responsibility for developing the drama to the group.	Meeting / Whole group in role.	You will take no nonsense - very assertive. Really push them to come up with a possible solution.

Whale

Based on the book 'My Friend Whale', by Simon James. [22]
Used with lower and upper primary, secondary, 16+, undergraduates, PGCE,
in-service, community.

Aim

To engage an inexperienced group in a piece of non-threatening drama.
To encourage an experienced group to use all their skills in matching content and
form to develop a drama.

Learning Outcomes		
Drama Skills	**Social Skills**	**Learning areas**
Belief in an imaginary situation - willing suspension of disbelief.	Work collaboratively.	Friendship.
Use of sound to create atmosphere.	Listen to other people's ideas and be sensitive in developing them.	Loss.
Sensitive questioning of a person in role and a chance to adopt a role.	Articulate a personal view point on a contentious subject.	Whales and their habitat. Environmental issues.
Sharing individual imagination to further the development of the whole class drama.	Use of a range of drama conventions.	Match form to content.

Contract

This drama requires a lot of imagination if it is to work. It is
about friendship, loss and the environment. I know the start of
the story but only to a certain point, after which we will need
to develop it together.

Game

Get the group to stand in a circle.

This is a game which depends upon us all helping each other. I
will demonstrate. "My name is ......[Allan] and I would like to
change places with my good friend..."

*Choose somebody, cross the circle, shake hands in the middle
and exchange places Play the game until everyone has had a
go. Different cultural greetings e.g. bow, salute, high five
could be used to vary the action.*

"What is a friend". Write down definitions offered. Take all suggestions and write them down verbatim.

We will return to these definitions at the end of our drama to see if we still agree with what we have just written.

Storytelling

Narrate the first sentence of the story.

There was once a boy *(or a girl, change pronouns as appropriate)* ...what should we call him? How old should he be?

Choose any age between five and twelve. Select a name and continue with the story using that name:

There was once a boy called........ who lived in a big city and was very happy because he had lots of friends. Then one day, just before the summer holidays his family moved to the coast. They moved to a house which was miles away from anywhere. The only other building anywhere near it was a lighthouse which stood on the rocks at the end of the cliffs.

He was the loneliest boy in the world. There was no one to play with, all his friends were back in the city and the summer holidays stretched out in front of him. He had nothing to do. Oh, how he missed his friends. He was so lonely that he couldn't even sleep. At nights he would get out of bed and go and look out of the window. He would climb on a stool and peer into the darkness. On a moonlit night even the toys in his bedroom looked lonely. He would look out across the bay at the stars and the moon and think about the good times he used to have.

At the end of the first week he was standing, as usual, looking out of the window late one night, when he saw something in the sea. He rubbed his eyes in disbelief, but it was still there. There, in the middle of his bay, was a whale! Its great tail rose above the water as it dived with a mighty splash.

He could not believe what he had seen. He watched and waited until it dived for the last time and then disappeared. There and then he made a plan. The next day when no one was looking he would get his swimming shorts, wrap them in a towel and put them under his bed. That night he would wait till everyone was asleep then reach under the bed, get his trunks and towel, look out of the window to check the whale had returned, tip-toe to his door, go carefully across the landing, down the stairs, open the outside door and go out into the night. He would make his way down the cliff path to the bay and go swimming in the same water as the whale! He lay down on his bed and was soon fast asleep, dreaming of tomorrow.

The next day he did exactly as planned. Nobody noticed a thing. That night he reached under the bed, and looked out of the window. Sure enough the whale was there! He tiptoed to his door, opened it slowly, carefully went across the landing, down the stairs and out through the door into the night. The pebbles crunched under his feet as he made his way down the cliff path to the bay. He put on his trunks and was soon swimming in the water.

And this is the most fantastic, incredible thing...he went swimming with the whale! He climbed on its back and the two of them went out to sea. As the whale dived he went down into a world he had never seen before. As they made their way across the shallow sands of the bay he saw broken bottles, cans and a few small fish. Then as the water deepened he saw an old shopping trolley, chains going down into the water, big containers with signs on them, a wreck and part of a car. As they swam further out into the ocean he saw something he just was not sure about.

One thing was for sure. By the time the whale turned round and headed back to the shore from the deeps, to the shallows of the bay, he had the best friend that anyone could ever have. He waved goodbye, put his pyjamas back on and made his way back up the cliff path to home. He quietly let himself in and was soon fast asleep.

The next day passed so quickly. He had to dry his towel and swimming trunks without anyone seeing and he had so much to think about that it was soon night time again and he was getting ready for his next swim. He wasn't lonely any more.

He went swimming with his friend the whale every night that week.

Saturday night came around and as usual he reached under the bed and got his towel and swimming trunks, tip-toed over to the window to check that his friend had arrived. But he couldn't see anything, there was no moon. He crossed the landing, went down the stairs, opened the door and went out into the night. It was very dark. He made his way down to the bay and the clouds lifted a little. The stars were out, but there was no sign of his friend.

He waited and waited until an hour had passed. He climbed up to the top of the cliff to get a better view of the sea, but still there was no sign. He was getting cold. He sat down, and with his towel clutched in his hands he pulled his knees in tightly to his chest. A boy under the stars on a cliff top waiting for his friend to arrive. He waited, and waited and waited but there was no sign of the whale.

Statement and Clarification

The last image we are left with is a small boy/girl on a cliff looking out to sea and waiting for his friend, the night is drawing in. Our drama is about what happens next between these two friends.

Collective Drawing

Before we find out what happens let us go back in time by one week to the first night......(name) goes swimming with whale. What did he see under the water?

Allow a re-cap

Some things he couldn't quite make out.

Split group in to smaller groups of 4/5.

What did he see that first night under the water? Draw this now, use your imagination.

This could be a quick exercise or a quality arts-based activity.

Discussion

Discuss the drawings, putting them together to form one large collage. Allow roles and places under the sea to emerge which may be useful in developing the drama later e.g.

Does the octopus you have drawn know the whale? Is the person that runs the underwater palace/factory friendly?

Soundscape/track, narration, director in role

We are moving closer to the final image of the story but are not quite there yet. Let us build up the situation on the night when the whale does not show up. Could you help create a soundscape/track for that very night when the child wakes up, goes to the window, then down to the bay and waits?

Model this as a director, get the group to quickly contribute sounds, keep the pace brisk. Either tape this or rehearse it, miming the action and narrating it yourself. Tension should be apparent.

Member of the group in role, soundtrack/scape, narration, artefact, mime/re-enactment

Would someone now take over the role ......[name] from me? All you have to do is mime to our sound track/tape. I will help you with narration.

Re-cap the sequence i.e. wake, look out of window, open door, past sleeping family, open outside door, into the night, to beach, watch, wait.

Discussion, hot seating, re-enactment, mime

Just before the re-enactment takes places ask the person playing the child

Would you mind answering some questions the group ask you as that child? You do not have to do anything other than answer as you would imagine that child would answer.

Ask the first question yourself as soon as the person sits e.g.

You must be cold, isn't it time you went home?

Model appropriate tone. Press gently for action to be taken, listen carefully to the group's ideas. Increase tension after a while by moving time on through narration e.g.

It's 3 o'clock now

and a minute later

It's 4 o'clock shouldn't we be going home?
etc.

At an appropriate point in the hot seating thank the role player and ask the group what the next scene should be. Select the suggestion with the most learning potential and/or dramatic possibilities. If there are many suggestions select elements of all of them and put them together in a sequence of action. Develop content and form together.

Branch Planning

- Use the ideas in the drawings to develop the drama. For example there may be a mermaid that the character could speak to. How would he get in touch with her? A letter? If someone has drawn something else, for example a submarine, build it and see who is on board, etc.

- The character gets in touch with all his old friends in the city. The class adopt these roles. How do they get away to the seaside? What do they do when they get there?

- The character is caught by their parents coming back into the house. What do the parents say. Improvisation in forum form. What have we learnt about the parent/s? Role on the wall.

- Have some whalers killed the whale? Steal a boat and chase after them. Teacher in role as captain of the whaling ship putting over the reasons why he has a right to kill these animals for his/her livelihood, etc.

- A private collector has captured the whale and put him/her in a sea zoo. Some of the class become sea zoo keepers, the other half the 'rescuers'. Newspaper stories about the way the whale is being confined, etc.

- The whale turns up late but needs help due to the environment beneath the waves being so polluted. Group metamorphose into the whale who then speaks to the character.

- Return to the ideas of 'friendship' written during discussion in step 3 and ask for any additions now having completed the drama. Have the group definitions deepened, broadened, changed, been reinforced?

Whale

	Step	Reason	Convention	Emphasis
1	Let the group know that this is a drama about friendship, loss and the environment. As the drama develops choices can be made about which dramatic avenues to follow. It is based on a fantastical story, but one which allows exploration of difficult issues.	To clarify the aims and prepare for the imaginative start of the drama.	Contract.	Just because things may appear fantastical this does not mean they cannot give us an insight into the material world.
2	In a circle start by saying "My name is .... and I would like to change places with my good friend ...... The individuals change places until everyone has had a go. Shake hands as you change places. Different cultural greetings could be used to vary the changes.	Places the concept of friendship firmly in focus.	Game.	Keep the "My name is ..." wording very clear and precise each time. If you know one person is likely to be left till last, ask them first.
3	Ask for definitions of a friend. Write them down.	To record initial understandings of 'friendship' and see if these have been expanded by the close of the work.	Discussion.	Take all definitions verbatim. There is no need to take these concepts early on eg. "Does not grass on me" does not have to become 'loyalty' yet.
4	Narrate the story of the child and the whale. Ask after the first line how old shall we make her/him, what shall we call her/him. Use that name in the story from that point onwards.	Choice of name and age allows the group to invest in the drama from the outset.	Storytelling.	The great friendship between the child and whale.
5	Clarify the last image of the story ie. a child alone on a small cliff top, towel under arm, the night all around, no sign of their friend. The drama is about what the child can do.	Focus the drama in terms of a problem to be solved.	Statement and clarification.	You do not know what this child will do from this point. However before the group explores this, it might be helpful to go back in time.

	Step	Reason	Convention	Emphasis
6	Split the whole group into smaller groups of 4/5. Go back to the first night the child swam with the whale. What did he see under the water? Draw 'things he couldn't quite make out'. Use your imagination (this can be a very quick exercise or a longer quality art-based activity.	Develops the imaginitive concept.	Collective drawing.	The whale has not yet 'disappeared', we are going back a week in time to that first night. You do not have to be able to draw well. It is the ideas we are looking for.
7	Discuss the drawings, asking who has drawn what, slowly allowing characters and places under the sea to emerge. (Put them together to form one large collage.)	To upgrade ideas presented visually and increase the sense of investment and ownership.	Discussion.	Upgrade all offerings; ask gently about characters in ways which challenge individuals to respond imaginatively eg. Does the octopus know the whale? or Is the person that runs this under water palace / factory friendly usually? Keep emphasising that this is *before* the whale has failed to appear.
8	Tell the group we are moving closer to the final image of the story but are not quite there yet. Could they help to create a soundscape / soundtrack for that very night when the child wakes up, goes to the window, than down to the bay and waits. Model this first as director. Listen to the tape when made. You don't have to tape it - it can just be repeated 'live'.	To build the context, increase tension, build to commitment.	Soundscape / soundtrack. Narration. Director in role.	We are still back in time on the night he goes and finds that the whale does not appear. Bring in sounds quickly. Keep this pacey and rough initially. It can be re-worked if necessary.
9	Ask if one of the group would take over your role. All they have to do is mime as you have done ie. Wake, look out of the window, go past sleeping family, out into the night, watch and wait. Tell them the tape will provide the back cloth.	To begin to draw in members of the group in role in the drama. Member of group in role.	Soundscape/track, Narration, Artefact, Mime/Re-enactment.	They can hardly go wrong. The rest of the group can also join in with the taped soundtrack/scape if they want or just watch. Use a towel as artefact.

Step	Reason	Convention	Emphasis
10 Just before the tape is replayed or live 'track' repeated, ask the person who has taken this role if they would mind answering a few questions as that child sat waiting for the whale.	To challenge the role and so increase ownership of this central character which is being handed over.	Discussion, Hot seating, Re-enactment, Mime.	The individual does not have to solve the question of where the whale is, just respond honestly. Could the rest of the group think of questions they might like to ask as the mime is being re-enacted.
11 Ask the first question yourself, to model a possible tone eg. call the child softly by his/her name and ask if they are feeling cold and is it not about time they were going home? Push after a while for the child to take some sort of action. 'What' is up to the child/group. Use narration to increase the tension eg. "It's 3 o'clock in the morning [name]" ..... after one minute. "It's 4 o'clock now .... had you not better do something?"	To give a depth, seriousness yet sense of fun to this phase of work. To upgrade comments and echo implications. To let everyone perhaps build belief etc.	Hot seating, Director as devil's advocate and legitimiser of questions. Narration.	If questions are sensitive, support them. Twist others that are not sensitive for implications. Eg. if someone says "Your mate's dead" then pick on it immediately and support it saying "Yes [name] you must have thought something terrible could have happened. Should you not do something to check now?"
12 Ask the group what the next scene could/should be. They could re-cap on all suggestions to date and the person playing the child could make a choice.	Hand over the discussions about content and form (if appropriate) to the class.	Discussion.	Focus on 'what' is the next scene and 'how' this could be structured to allow everyone to participate. Sequence a number of scenes if many are suggested and have potential.

Crash Landing

Used with upper primary, secondary, 16+, undergraduates, PGCE, in service, community.

Aim

To provide opportunities for whole group work and in various sub-groups.

Learning Outcomes		
Drama Skills	**Social Skills**	**Learning areas**
Work together as part of a whole group to devise work and re-create key moments in a variety of forms	Take part in whole group decision making	Democracy
Adopt, sustain and develop a role	Problem solving	Violence
Use space imaginatively	Survival	Use mime skills

Resources

Paper, felt pens, crayons, cloak, tape player, cassette with 'battle music', eg. 'Achilles last stand' by Led Zepplin.

Narration

Lie on the floor and close your eyes. Heels together, arms by your side. Roll your head from side to side until it comes to rest in a comfortable position.

It is a Saturday morning, and you are sitting having a cup of tea. You hear the post arrive. You pick it up and discover a letter addressed to you. You open it, and can't believe your eyes. You have won a competition, a free two week holiday in the Caribbean, all expenses paid. The week until you go passes in a blur. Lots of shopping, some new clothes, sort out your passport, sun tan lotion, a new suitcase. Before you know it the day you leave is here. The taxi blows its horn, you put your cases in the boot, and you are off speeding down the motorway to the airport. You check your bags in, and go through to the departure lounge. A free cup of coffee, and then you're walking up the stairs to the aircraft. You get a window seat, no smoking, of course. The 'fasten your seat belt' signs come on. The engines roar, the brakes come off, and you shoot into the air. Looking down, everything looks like toy town, the tiny fields, the tiny cows and cars. You level off at 35,000 feet, seat belts off. You relax into your seat. The food arrives and you get one of those lovely little meals in the plastic containers. You are relaxed and full, you recline your seat and nod off. Hours later you are rudely awoken by a lurch in the plane. You seem to be being thrown everywhere. The captain's voice comes over the intercom. "Sorry, ladies and gentlemen, we have run into an electrical storm, please fasten your seat belts. We are going to try to fly above it". Lightning flashes all around you. Suddenly there is a massive flash of lightning. You look out of the window and see that the plane has been hit. Flames flash everywhere. The plane starts to career downwards alarmingly, you know you are going to crash, the last thing you remember is the captain saying "Ladies and gentlemen, please adopt the position for crash landing...."

When I clap my hands you are going to wake up. You have been washed up on the beach of a desert island. You have survived. When I clap my hands the action will start.

Whole Group in Role (with teacher in role as survivor)

Let the play run. You may need to stop it fairly soon and clarify role and situation. Ask questions such as,

"Where will you sleep?" "What will you eat?" "How will you keep warm?"

You could do this in role -

"Don't we need to build a shelter?"

Try to keep the status of the role low.

Define Space

Within the role ask them to build a shelter, a fire etc. This can last as long as you think necessary.

Small Group Improvisation

In small groups I want you to prepare an improvisation where you explore the island.

Show and discuss

Map Making

When they have shown this, get them all around you, and draw the outline of the island on a large piece of paper. Each group is to declare what they found and this is to be drawn on to the map. Try and emphasise features which could be good for drama such as caves, uncrossable rivers, abandoned mines, ancient relics, etc.

Whole Group in Role

Again let the play run - see where they take it. The following are suggestions which you might want to fold into the drama.

Teacher in Role

Use costume if possible - a large black cape can work. Enter at a good moment and demand,

"What do you think you are doing on my island?"

What follows is the gist of what you need to get over.

I am the great Kaliber - magician of the Ancient world - granted this island for eternity

You are in great danger, for within 3 days the monster will surface and then you will surely perish in the fight between him and me.

Several years ago I became lonely and made myself a companion. He was kind and loyal, and we were great friends. However, after a while he grew restless. He became jealous of my powers. He became so bitter that in the end he broke into my study and stole my spell book. He cast spells and turned himself into a monster. He tried magic on-me and after a 3 day battle I managed to overpower him. I cast a huge spell which entombed him underground. However, every ten years the spell wears off and he is free. Then I have to face him again. He will surface in 3 days

Clarification

Ask them, out of role, if they have any questions.

Designing

In groups (4-6) draw a picture of what you think the monster looks like. Show them - choose one.

Teacher in Role

To help you escape before the big battle I will give you a gift. Take these three pieces of 'Splodge'. Who will be the guardians?

Mime giving a piece of putty type substance to 3 of the group.

Splodge can be turned into anything you want in the world. All you have to do is shape it, say Splodge 3 times and it will be real. However it will only work if everyone in the group agrees and you all say Splodge 3 times. Now I must go to prepare for the battle. Farewell, good luck, and choose carefully.

Discussion may well be how to use the Splodge. You may need to intervene and reinforce the need for all to agree. Usually the first piece of splodge is used to make a form of transport to leave the island. Again small groups designing and then choosing can be effective.

Enter the transport and leave the island.

Narration

As we left the island there was the terrifying sound of the earth being ripped apart. From the heart of the island the monster emerged. Kaliber appeared, and stood resolutely before it.

Dance

I want you to split into two groups. Listen to this music.

Play a piece suitable for the battle

Devise a class dance piece to represent the battle.

Branch Planning

Whole Group in Role
If they escape from the island, you will have to make up a story together i.e. Where they go and what they do with the splodge.

Crash Landing

	Step	Reason	Convention	Emphasis
1	Tell them a story to get them onto island.	A quick and efficient way to establish role and situation.	Narration.	Use tone of voice to make it exciting where appropriate.
2	Let the play begin where we wake up.	They begin to explore role and situation.	Whole group in role / Teacher in role / Define space.	Be aware the group may need to stop and clarify.
3	Explore the island.	Establish ownership of the space / island.	Small group improvisation.	Show geography of the island through speech and movement.
4	Let's draw the areas we have been to.	Make concrete the imagination.	Map making.	Try to build in features which have drama potential.
5	Let the play run.	A chance to establish all the groundwork done so far.	Whole group in role.	Be prepared to go with their ideas.
6	Enter as Kaliber.	Challenge the group.	Teacher in role, clarification.	Costume is important.
7	Draw a picture of the monster.	Through experience arrive at a common vision.	Designing.	Stress the need to present your design well.
8	Give them the Splodge.	A device to get them all to agree before they can proceed.	Teacher in role.	They must all agree. One person can veto any decision.
9	How is the Splodge to be used? Choose a form of transport.	To get them to arrive at an agreed decision with a common focus.	Whole group in role, Designing.	Everyone involved should have a say. Again stress the need to present designs well.
10	The monster emerges.	Moves the story on.	Narration.	They are merely to be spectators.
11	Recreate the conflict through movement.	Show conflict without using violence.	Dance.	Half the group could represent the monster, the other half Kaliber.
12	What happens next?	To feel the freedom of their role.	Whole group in role.	The rest is up to them.

Beauty and the Beast

Used with upper primary, secondary, 16+, undergraduates, PGCE, in-service, community.

Aim

To explore the issue of stereotyping through a well known story and give the group a chance to experiment with a range of conventions.

Learning Outcomes		
Drama Skills	**Social Skills**	**Learning areas**
Try out different and unorthodox approaches in experimenting with improvisation.	Work in a variety of groupings	Appearances and expectations
Demonstrate a knowledge of focus and tension.	Express personal ideas in a public forum.	Nurture/nature beliefs, values and attitudes.
Explore the use of symbol and metaphor.	Negotiation.	Love.
Use a range of appropriate conventions in a prepared performance.		

Resources

Old parchment with the words "Take anything you want, but nothing take away" (A piece of oven baked paper, stained with a tea bag and covered in talcum powder looks authentic), a rose (plastic/real/paper), an item of costume to signify the Beast, a necklace, a bracelet.

Contract and Definition of Space

As the group enters, set out the chairs in the room in a large horseshoe shape. Group sit in the chairs. They are asked to join in a drama of a well known story. This will start with the practitioner telling her version but will end up with the class producing their own version. At various points there will be the opportunity to bring parts of the story to life.

This will help us build our own story once the tale has been told and the drama begins. In other words we will work through the 'text' and see what work we would like to do in response as we work together on this project. Come and sit round me for the beginning of it, we will sit on the floor. You are now sitting in the set for part of our drama.

Storytelling / Narration

The rain beat hard against the merchant as he rode at full gallop into the night. As he rode, the horse carried him swiftly along the road home from the port to the village where he lived but it seemed a long, long way this night. All his ships had been sunk without trace at sea and instead of riding home with treasures he was making his way empty handed with all lost and nothing to hope for.

As he rode he thought of his wife and how she would scold and mock him for making her a laughing stock in front of the rest of the village. All the neighbours would be already gathered around at their house to celebrate even as he rode. He was so distressed he began to speak out aloud to himself. He thought about his eldest daughter and how she would scorn him for not having bought her the pearl necklace he promised, and his second daughter who would get so angry at the loss of the rich ruby bracelet she had been promised. Then he thought of his youngest daughter and how her heart would be broken at his misfortune. She asked for nothing save her father's love and perhaps a single rose as a sign of his affection. The wind carried his tumbled, distressed words away but his mind was as troubled as ever.

Suddenly the horse reared up, there was a clap of thunder, a flash of lightning and the merchant found himself being carried wildly into the woods that lay to the side of the road. No path, just trees, the sound of hooves in mud and on rock as they tore further and further away from the road. Then all went quiet. He sat upright and the horse cantered on to a cobbled yard that lay in front of a castle. The wind had dropped completely, 'That's odd, I'm sure I've never seen the castle before and I have ridden this road many times', thought the merchant.

He dismounted and tied the horse. "Hello," he called. All was still. "Hello," no reply. He went up the stone steps and pushed gently on the studded wooden door. Gargoyles lined a long corridor. As he headed slowly down, it was as though a hundred eyes were staring at him, but the moment he looked back, they turned to stone again. By the time he got to the end of the passage he was so relieved that he pushed open the door that lay in front of him almost with a shove.

Still image / Game / Re-enactment

Ask the participants to form 2 lines to try and reconstruct the merchant's walk up the corridor.

From the moment I enter the corridor I must see only stone faces/gargoyles but I must sense that when I turn away/turn back that the faces with 'a hundred eyes' are looking at me.
Here is where I will enter, here is where I shove open the door at the end of the corridor.

Point to two ends of the room along which a double sided corridor of standing participants can be formed.

To build atmosphere this may have to be repeated but is done in the form of a game. e.g.

I caught you moving then....... let's try again

Lights may also be dimmed and a cloak could be effectively used for the merchant here to create atmosphere and build belief.

Discussion / Questioning

Ask the participants now to sit in the previously arranged seats.

How do you think the merchant is feeling now?

Responses given.

Storytelling / Narration

..... he pushed open the door that lay in front of him. It swung back to reveal a hall with a ceiling so high that he was not sure if it had a roof. A fire was roaring in the grate though and a table was set with plates and covered dishes everywhere. "Hello", he called again, walking to the top of the table, hoping to meet his host. Huge paintings were on the walls, tapestries hung down, suits of armour, carved figures, animals' heads looked down and at him, watching his every move.

Metamorphosis / Define space / Small group work

Choose a place for yourself in this huge hall. We know the table is down the middle. Get into a position where you can watch the merchant. You could be a figure in a painting, in a suit of armour, a carving an animal's head - you choose, you can use your chair if you like.

Allow time for this, the group can work in pairs, 3/4s or individually.

Defining space, Modelling / Artefact

Ask participants to sit down in the great hall.
Move from one individual or group to another and ask them to show their tableau/frozen image/still picture. The rest of the group guess. If they can't get it the individual or group lets them know. The focus moves to each group briefly.

Before you go into role as the merchant walk through the route you will take past the figures, paintings etc. and place an old piece of parchment covered in dust on a chair at the head of the 'table'. On it are the words "TAKE ANYTHING YOU WANT, BUT NOTHING TAKE AWAY".

Re-enactment / Narration

The narration is re-wound from 'He pushed open the door that lay in front of him.....'

In addition, weave into the narrative references to the things in the room that the group have created. Continue with this narrative.

At the head of the table he found a place set, as though someone was expecting a guest or about to dine alone. Had someone invited him here to eat he wondered? Then on the table on top of one of the silver covers he saw a note. The ink was still wet on it, but the dust was thick. He blew and as the dust settled he read: "Take anything you want, but nothing take away". He read it again, "Take anything you want but nothing take away". It did not make sense. Unless...... Unless it meant that he was to eat his fill, take warmth from the fire and shelter from the cruel night, but then be on his way leaving the treasures of the castle intact. He was tired and hungry and thought this must be so and in thinking so he lifted the first lid and "bing" a huge pie and "bing" a plateful of steaming new potatoes, his favourite vegetable. Then another lid, "bing", buttered carrots, "bing" gravy and then he just thought of his thirst when, "bing", a decanter of wine, "bing", and a mug of foaming ale. And you can imagine that the merchant ate everything. He "binged" until he could "bing" no more.

Full, warm and strangely refreshed, the merchant knew he must leave the warmth of the great hall and journey again into the night. If only he could thank his magical host and promise when his fortunes were better that he would repay the tremendous kindness shown to him. He pushed his chair under the table, looked at the fire that was roaring as warmly as when he had just entered and walked back down the hall. His clothes were dry now and he noticed all that he had missed in his misery and fear when he had first entered. Down the sides of the great hall beneath the tapestries were cupboards and chests and tables overflowing with jewels and treasures from all over the world. There was a whole chest full of pearl necklaces just like the one he had promised his eldest daughter, there was a whole drawer full of ruby bracelets just like the one he had promised his second daughter. But so honest was the merchant, and so grateful for the kindness that he had received he would not repay a generous host in such a way. He closed the great door behind him and walked down the corridor of gargoyles where once again he felt that these stone eyes were staring at him as he passed.

Thought tracking / teacher in role / handing over role

Ask the participants to move in to a horseshoe shape again and then pass behind the merchant and speak his thoughts. Put the cloak on a chair to represent the merchant.

Would someone take on this role? Do you need to know anything else about the merchant?

If she/he does, then the merchant can be hot seated. If the individual who takes over the role is committed, hand it over, for the rest of the drama. If not, hold on to it yourself for a while and play both roles which follow.

I am going to carry on with the story from the moment he steps into the courtyard in the moonlight. Here is your horse, there is the castle. Which is the way home? You are going to have to think quickly and listen carefully. One other task - you don't speak in this scene, not a word - you will see why. Everyone else who is watching, try to pick up clues about what is happening and we will discuss them after the scene has finished.

The merchant was about to swing onto the horse's back when something caught his eye. There, in the middle of the courtyard grew a single rose.

Move to the middle of the horseshoe and hold up a rose (artificial or real). It should be produced as if from nowhere, 'magically' as in the story.

Strange, he had not seen it when he had arrived. He reached across and before he realised what he had done, he snapped it from its stalk for his youngest daughter.

Break quietly away to the open end of the horseshoe, and put on a mask/costume/symbolic representation, continue with the narration.

"How dare you!" The voice was terrible and dark and he spun round. There in front of him stood a creature, half man and half beast, that made him cringe with fear and revulsion. "I give you everything I have. You take it and then take more. Did you not read. 'Take anything you want but nothing take away'. Did I not give you food, warmth, shelter. You repay me by killing my rose. How can it every grow again. You will give me something. Now it is my turn to take. By tomorrow night you will leave your youngest daughter here with me. If she is not here with me by sunset both you and she and all your family will die".

A cloud came across the light of the moon and all went dark. When the merchant tried to speak he found himself alone in the moonlight. He climbed on his horse and rode as fast as he could through the trees, on to the road and back to the village. Everyone was waiting for him and the door opened.

| Thought tracking |

Ask the participant who played the merchant to stand and let the others pass in a circle behind him/her and decide from them all what he is really thinking. Model this e.g.

How did he know about my daughter?

and explain that the same questions can and will be asked. Take your place in the circle as one of the group.

Ask the person playing the role what she feels about all that has been said to her - taking care to highlight those points which may have emerged as being of most interest to the group (a searching for contextual subtexts).

Small group work / Teacher in role

Set a task to be worked on in groups. Split the participants into groups of 5 to show what the merchant does from the moment he is standing in the moonlight to the deadline of sunset that day i.e. approx. 16 hours.

You can be any character you like, teacher, mother, 3 sisters, villagers but not the beast as the drama is only going up to the point before sunrise. In terms of the story the merchant is expected at home, his family and the villagers are waiting, the door has just opened

To improvise this part of the story you must use at least five of the previous techniques and conventions we have used so far.

1 Narration
   e.g. telling the story - could be used at the beginning of our story .
2 Still Pictures
   e.g. in the great hall.
3 Mime
   e.g. Merchant and the beast
4 Re-enactment
   e.g. The merchant going down the corridor
5 Thought tracking
   e.g. The merchant's thoughts
6 Defining space
   e.g. The shape of the great hall
7 Hot seating
   e.g. As we did to the merchant to find out more.
8 Taking on more than one role
   e.g. Teacher as merchant and beast.
9 Costuming
   eg. Cloak/beast clothes/mask.
10 Artefacts
   eg. Parchment and dust/paper and powder, rose.

The piece must be no longer than 3 minutes. Conventions help us move through time!

When you present your prepared improvisation of the time between moonlight and sunset you must be prepared to improvise spontaneously from the point where the beast appears. Do not anticipate or plan this. I will behave as I think the beast would. You too must be true to the roles you have created. You cannot fix anything up with me. This is part of the task, I will be coming around and will listen in.

Time is allowed for good preparation of these improvisations. Walk around and listen in so as to decide how to challenge from within the drama and perhaps to clarify the task.

Small group prepared improvisation challenged by teacher in role

Each group re-enacts their prepared improvisation. Enter in role at the end of each. Co-ordinate feedback on each improvisation and the way the group structured it.

Branch Planning

The practitioner asks the group where they would like to go from this point. She asks them to think in terms of form and content e.g.

Story Telling / Narration

This is what happened in my version of the story.

The door opened. Out came his daughters and all the villagers. "Look my pearl necklace", "Look my ruby bracelet", "Oh my husband and all the wealth you have bought with you". And as he looked down he saw his horse was indeed laden with treasure and in his hand he held a single rose. "I don't understand," he said. "Bring the treasures". His wife and the villagers carried him in, but as they danced and sang and made merry the merchant just sat and looked at the single rose in his hand. It all came back to him. "Stop." He shouted. "Stop you don't realise. Stop." - "He is tired," said his wife. "Don't annoy our guests." "There is a terrible price to pay," he shouted. But everyone ignored him. Only his youngest daughter saw the trouble in his eyes and asked him what she could do. "Unless I give you away forever to a beast then you and I, your mother and sisters will all surely die." "But father will you give me away?" "I have promised." "Yes but will you do so?" "No," he said.

No sooner had he uttered the word "No" than screams rang out. "Aagh... my necklace is burning me!" screamed the eldest daughter. "Aagh my bracelet is eating into my arm," cried the other sister. "Aagh," screamed the guests, "The treasures are like acid to touch." And the single rose leapt on to the fire and danced as the beast's image appeared in the flames, "Tomorrow by sunset", then faded into the fire which, "snap", went dead. And in that cold house when all the guests had speedily left, there was nothing to be heard but the sound of whimpering.

Only the youngest daughter had the courage to speak. "Father, I will go at sunset. All I ask is that you take me there to the place I must meet the beast and then go. Father do you understand?" His eyes filled with tears as he looked up at his daughter and nodded his head. That evening before sunset they set off and sooner than either of them would have wished climbed down off their horses in the castle courtyard.

Relationship wheel /thought tracking

Let us set the scene in the home. You all know the merchant. Will you be the merchant? Will you be the first daughter, you the second and you the third? Would you be the merchant and go and stand in the centre of the horseshoe. The rest of the class - think who you would like to be in the village. Go and stand in relation to the merchant in turn as we move around the circle. e.g. near him if you get on well with him, far away if you dislike him. In a moment I am going to ask you individually what you think about the merchant at this point in the action. When I tap you on the shoulder speak your thoughts out loud.

Analogy

In small groups the group work on performances of either the traditional story ending or their own version.

Beauty and the Beast

	Step	Reason	Convention	Emphasis
1	Set the chairs in a horse-shoe shape.	Defines the space for drama.	Contract / Define space.	This is one version of Beauty and the Beast. We will use it as a starting point to create our own.
2	Bring the group into the middle of the 'horse-shoe' and tell the story up until the merchant has walked the length of the passage.	Hook interest, provide a clear situation, focal role, perspective and focus.	Storytelling.	Stress the worry and despair of the merchant.
3	Group become gargoyles and faces in the corridor wall.	To use the tension of this game to increase involvement.	Still image / Game / Re-enactment.	The merchant must not see the faces moving.
4	How do you think the merchant is feeling now?	To clarify his predicament.	Discussion / Questioning.	Build sympathy for the merchant.
5	Tell story up to entrance into the large hall.	To increase tension.	Storytelling.	The fire roaring through the grate though the building seems deserted.
6	In a small group create a still image as an object in the Great Hall. Show and discuss these.	Use imagination to create set and atmosphere.	Metamorphosis / Define space / Small group work.	Give examples eg. figures in a painting.
7	Tell the story, discover the parchment. Pupil as merchant.	To create expectancy.	Define space / Artefact / Modelling.	Repeat the words written on the parchment as if pondering on them.
8	Rewind the narrative with the previous group work included.	To build tension.	Re-enactment / Narration.	The surprise and amazement of the merchant.

	Step	Reason	Convention	Emphasis
9	Pass behind the merchant and speak his thoughts in the first person.	To increase pressure on the merchant.	Thought tracking / Teacher in role / Handing over of role.	Repeat some of the thoughts suggested.
10	Continue with the story and the re-enactment of it up until the point the merchant arrives back in his village.	To set the central dilemma.	Re-enactment / Teacher in role / Narration / Costume.	The person playing the role of the merchant reacts but does not speak. This needs to be controlled through the narrative.
11	Pass behind the merchant and speak his thoughts in the first person.	To clarify the situation the merchant is in.	Thought tracking.	The merchant has indeed broken the rules of hospitality.
12	Split into groups of 5 and show what the merchant does from that moment until sunset that day.	To prepare a rehearsed improvisation which increases the tension of the next spontaneous encounter.	Small group work.	The passage of approximately 16 hours needs to be shown. How can the drama conventions used so far help you translate your ideas into a satisfying dramatic form? It cannot involve the beast. No longer than 3 minutes.
13	Challenge this via teacher in role.	To consider different dramatic solutions.	Teacher in role / Small group improvisation.	Co-ordinate feedback from each group's improvisation so that all ideas are valued.
14	Each group re-enacts its improvisation. The teacher enters in role at the end of each and a resolution is improvised.	To challenge understanding in terms of interest and facilitate discussion of form.	Small group prepared improvisation challenged by teacher in role.	Be sensitive to the level of challenge in role and in discussion of forms used.

ASSESSING AND EVALUATING DRAMA WORK

When we say, "Sam Smith is good at drama" what do we mean? How do we communicate this to Sam in a way which will help her/him to identify what has to be done to become " very good at drama"? The reason why we assess and evaluate is to allow for the possibility of improvement in individual levels of skills, knowledge and understanding. This immediately raises the concepts of development and progression and the need to consider practical mechanisms which allow this to be assessed, evaluated, monitored, recorded and reported.

But before looking at the 'how' of assessment and evaluation it might be helpful to consider the question of **what** we feel it is important to assess and evaluate in Drama. A practitioner's planning, assessment and evaluation procedures will reveal a great deal about what she values in teaching and learning.

Clarification of personal values in relation to education and drama can help determine the approach which suits you and your group in your particular context. For example, you may disagree with these statements, but we believe:

- in involving the individual in identifying and making sense of what they have learned

- that becoming better in process drama involves becoming a creative, adaptable, flexible, resilient, balanced individual who can work and play alone as well as with others

- that good process drama practice is often driven by the search for important questions rather than the re-statement of perceived truths. In this sense process drama practitioners value expressions of 'articulate uncertainty' and seek to question rigid positions of inarticulate and articulate certainty.

- that some of the most important things in drama cannot be assessed, though they can be evaluated e.g. 'communitas'[23] - the feeling of community which can come from engagement with the art form, e.g. 'metaxis'[24] - the ability to hold the world of fiction next to our own worldview, the comfort or disturbance this can generate and the potential of this to affect our everyday realities and actions.

- in process drama the experience itself is sometimes more important than showing it to others, though the ability to reflect in order to monitor one's own progress is critical. In this sense assessing skills and information learnt is not any more important than evaluating engagement

- the teaching of drama and theatre skills do not necessarily have priority over personal and social development

- in the social reconstructionist tradition of education[25] which defines both schooling and teacher education as critical elements in a move towards a just society and places emphasis on preparing teachers to think critically about the social order

- there is no causal link between one drama methodology and quality learning[26]

- that a prescribed, content-heavy drama curriculum can be restrictive e.g. 'by the age of 11 students should have been introduced to basic dramatic forms, such as comedy, tragedy, and farce, as well as to a variety of European and non-European theatre styles, and should be able to recognise these forms when confronted by them [27].

- a good drama practitioner is intuitive and follows hunches rather than mechanically following lesson plans in order to deliver pre-determined learning outcomes. This involves acting on evidence from assessment (formal and informal) to enable individual pupils to progress

- differentiation in drama is a process, which involves the practitioner responding to the different outcomes from the tasks set. Responding with specific resources is just one aspect over which we have control

- assessment should focus on what an individual can do, rather than what they cannot do (deficit model) and should be criterion referenced

- any method of monitoring, assessment, evaluation, recording and reporting should be driven by the desire to motivate the practitioner and the group rather than the need to be accountable which can quickly sap energies.

- good drama practitioners evaluate their own practice as they assess individual and group progress and this process is integral to the way they work

- assessment should be the servant and not the master of the curriculum [28].

From the above statement of our values, you can perhaps see why we plan as we do. In the pretexts "aims" and "learning objectives" are identified but they remain 'possible' not 'certain'. The structure of a pretext, and subsequent sessions, can of course, ensure that there is an opportunity to develop skills (e.g. skilled use of gesture in performance) and acquire knowledge in drama (e.g. knowledge about a specific genre such as agit-prop). It can allow for the development of specific social skills (e.g. the ability to support other people's ideas). It can also encourage consideration of other learning areas with significance beyond the drama classroom, studio or space (e.g. justice, loss, and friendship). We set expressive learning objectives where the tasks individuals will engage with are specified rather than instructional objectives which identify specific skills and information that are to be learnt[29]. This allows the practitioner and all members of the group, whatever their ability, the opportunity to explore learning that is important to them. To predict or even pre-determine such learning as a result of engagement with drama (or any other art form) can be restrictive, perhaps impossible.

Why is Assessment and Evaluation Such a Controversial Matter in Drama Education?

The issues of assessment and evaluation of drama work have undoubtedly led to much consternation and heated verbal exchanges between practitioners over the years. Why are they such controversial issues in this field? Essentially, because any one set of assessment and evaluation procedures will be based on a specific set of selected criteria which must be wittingly, or unwittingly based on a system of values. The imposition of any one system can be seen to negate legitimate work generated from a totally different set of criteria and the values implicit within these. As we have argued, it is not, in other words, just the 'how' of assessment in drama that is at the root of disagreements but fundamentally, the 'what?'

Any attempt to devise assessment and evaluation schemes for drama education also reveals the rich paradoxes within the subject.

"Drama and theatre are paradoxical, in order to liberate they must captivate. They teach by leading up the garden path." [30].

In order to captivate the interest, enthusiasm and commitment of many young people and adults, the drama practitioner must be able to draw upon as wide a range of approaches and methodologies as possible. This is also true for a group as it develops in the long term. It is the practitioner's job to motivate, challenge and provide stimulation and creative inputs at key points in a group's development. Then comes the sticking point. To what end is the practitioner using the art form to captivate? For example, listed below are three garden paths which practitioners have often led group members up in the past.

The first is that of drama skills and knowledge. For example, in terms of skills, the ability to sustain and develop a role or to use contrast to effect. In terms of knowledge, for example, to know how chorus was used in Greek tragedy and how it has been used to effect by a variety of contemporary playwrights or companies.

Another is the path of personal and social skills; in personal skills, for example, the ability to develop confidence and resilience. In social skills for example, to develop the abilities and skills needed to work in a group, to challenge other people's ideas constructively and work with them whilst also being able to put forward personal viewpoints.

A third path is that leading to other learning areas beyond the studio, classroom or other space. For example, gaining insight into concepts such as 'justice' at one end of the scale, concrete facts at the other e.g. cruelty to children, facts from the NSPCC. One label that has been given to this pathway is that of drama as a learning medium, or more recently, applied drama.

In reality of course the three paths often run side by side or cross each other through design or by coincidence.

It is a relatively straightforward matter to formulate a set of assessment criteria for the teaching and learning of drama skills and knowledge. For example, some of these already exist within the National Curriculum English Orders for children aged 5-16 in England [31]. There is also a choice between GCSE and 'A' Level Examination Boards which allows individual practitioners to select an examination that they feel realistically addresses the type and amount of drama skills and knowledge appropriate for their students. Difficulties arise when we consider the question of introducing an agreed knowledge and skill base of theatre arts content and criteria in the whole 5-18 curriculum on a national basis. This automatically raises the question of 'what' knowledge and 'when' it should be introduced. Attempts have been made at this but they invariably result in an over-prescribed, content-saturated drama programme. For example:

'By the age of 9 or 10, students should be able to grasp the basic ingredients of dramatic narrative-tension, conflict, surprise, plot development and resolution - have a fair idea of drama's historical and cultural diversity.' [32]

Just because it is not possible to present a set of national criteria to assess personal and social learning or the effect drama can have on an individual's perceptions does not mean that these aspects of drama are not important. This difficulty is currently mirrored in the world of contemporary postmodern performance:

John Freeman points directly to this when he states that:

'instruction and assessment... owe more to historical drama school vocationality than to contemporary practice... it remains a central, though at times crumbling, distinction, after all, that drama schools focus on the 'how' and academic institutions prioritise the 'why' of performance... With work, which often offers an absence of applaudable skill, how do we differentiate between the good and the bad?' [33]

Having stated that what is to be assessed is the 'why' of performance, specific criteria now have to be generated. The difficulty of course comes in finding a method, or range of methodologies which 'fairly' assess the extent to which a student has progressed in understanding concepts related to the 'why' of performance. Even when these have been established it does not prevent other practitioners in the same institution or others arguing that this is not really what studying drama at university level is all about, or that at least the students should also know and be trained to a reasonable level in the 'how' and knowledge of those who have explored these 'hows' before them. The same criticisms are applied to some forms of drama in schools, and a whole range of community settings.

There are bound to be differences about the 'what' to assess as different teachers and schools view drama and theatre in different ways and this is a healthy sign that the context is informing the form of work. For example one institution may feel that social and personal learning and drama and theatre skills are the most important and viable areas of learning to set criteria in. Another might feel that the emphasis should be placed firmly on drama and theatre knowledge and skills and another that it will try and balance both these areas of learning.

There has been a plea from some practitioners to stop a 'lop-sidedness' developing when it comes to balancing required skills and knowledge with intangibles such as personal and social, spiritual and moral development. They argue that all we can really assess in drama is the participant's ability to do drama. The difficulty with this argument comes when, for example, a school or teacher is committed to a progressive, child/person centred education system and considers this aspect of the work to be most deserving of their efforts. In this scenario the assessable knowledge and skills acquired through drama are important but secondary to the intangible, but nonetheless perceived developments in terms of personal, social and general learning areas. In other words, there are aspects of drama which are crucial but difficult to assess and the danger is that we:
    "...make the measurable important rather than the important measurable'. [34]

Since the advent of the Educational Reform Act of 1988 [35] drama in the UK has continued to grow and be practised in the secondary sector. This is perhaps surprising in that it was not a named National Curriculum foundation subject. The numbers of pupils taking drama is growing, and being defended in the face of pressure to reduce subjects on the timetable [36]. This is arguably not because of the drama skills and knowledge it provides but because of the totally un-assessable perceived and felt values of the subject to the vast majority of its pupils in personal, social, moral, cultural and spiritual terms [37].

Content alone does not determine the level of work taught and learnt. We believe that any pretext can be taught to any age or ability range. It is the approach to the work that is of crucial importance. This means, for example, that in many cases the same key tasks can be given to Year 5 pupils as to students with Firsts in Theatre Arts, as to prisoners who have never done drama in their lives. Of course these key tasks would be framed in slightly different ways so as to be age and ability appropriate and the level of resourcing, support, response and expectations of outcome would be very different.

So for example in the 'King Lear' pretext a year five group would work very much from their imagination in creating costumes from paper and would relate their interpretation of character loosely to this. A group of students with Firsts in Theatre Arts would engage in the same activity but there would be an expectation that the interpretation of character through costume on a symbolic and metaphorical level could be articulated and grounded in a wide frame of reference, exhibiting detailed knowledge of the text. There would also be high expectations in terms of the actual technical and professional construction of the costume. A group of prisoners would engage with the same text, at least ostensibly, but the emphasis would be on enabling them to locate a subtext that had particular resonance for them at that moment in time e.g. the need to hide true feelings in order to survive.

Before we look at range of drama assessment methods it is perhaps worth checking what the practitioner of drama might reasonably be expected to be responsible for and then establishing some key definitions.

Definitions and Responsibilities

First of all what should the teacher of drama be responsible and accountable for in terms of assessment and evaluation? This definition by HMI is helpful in setting the context.

The teacher with responsibility for drama needs to formulate a scheme of work, which outlines the drama practice in the school...This scheme should set down aims, learning objectives, teaching methods, evaluation and assessment procedures and a record keeping system. It should foster progression through the years and contribute to the progression across the different phases of education, reflecting both the range of pupil ability and the wider social context of the school and its community [38].

The link between schemes of work/pretexts and assessment, evaluation, recording and reporting procedures is strongly made. There is also emphasis on the function of assessment, which is to be:

'the vehicle of communication in helping both teacher and pupils to evaluate their work.' [39]

It is important that any such procedures should be written in clear, comprehensible language so that pupils, the teacher, parents and the wider community can take informed decisions about future action based on the extent of the achievements [40]. To use a well-worn phrase the assessment process should continually provide both *'feedback and feed forward'* [41]. Let us first be clear about the definitions we are using. We need to tell the participants what they are going to be doing - then evaluate what they did, from this they need to formulate individual targets to make sure they are clear about what they need to do next in order to improve the quality of their work.

Assessment:

The major function of assessment in drama is to provide information about pupils abilities and levels of attainment in specified areas of skills, knowledge and understanding. These do not all have to be specified before work takes place, some will arise during the work and others will legitimately be acknowledged retrospectively. If a student knows what she is good at and what she needs to develop then a statement about progress has been made which gives feedback and feed forward, otherwise progress is merely a matter of chance.

There are three main purposes for and functions of assessment:

1 **Diagnostic** which analyses what a pupil is capable of and/or learning difficulties so that guidance can be provided
2 **Summative** which records overall achievement at the end of a piece of work
3 **Formative** which focuses on identifying progress being made in order to plan the next steps for development

Evaluation:

The major function of evaluation in drama is to review methods of work and quality of provision. However, assessment and evaluation are two related processes. For example, agreed assessment procedures are needed to allow meaningful evaluation to take place. On the other hand because assessments of pupils can not be statements of absolute ability 'they can only be statements about achievements within the framework of educational opportunities that have been provided' [42] every assessment must, in some degree, be related to an evaluation of the teacher and the school/institution. The quality of teaching and the quality of learning are in this sense inter-linked.

Aims:

what the individual practitioner intends to do e.g. To explore the concept of 'friendship' and to engage an inexperienced group in a piece of non-threatening drama.

Learning outcomes:

what individuals will be given the opportunity to do. These will embody different objective types [43] e.g.

- instructional - which specifies skills and information to be learnt: learn about whales and their habitat
- expressive - does not specify what is to be learnt but defines a task in which they are to engage, or a situation in which they are to work, such as adopt a role and interact with others in role.

In pre-determining certain learning outcomes the practitioner is simply devising specific activities that will enable her aims to be achieved. It is often the case that overall progress is ensured by having a clear and simple set of aims for a series of lessons, together with a larger range of stated learning outcomes to achieve these.

Progression:

The process of education has the aim of changing people and their behaviour by imparting skills, increasing knowledge and understanding and developing competencies.' [44].

If there is evidence of this happening then there is progression.

This is a dynamic process in which individuals are constantly developing. It is important for teachers to be aware of the levels reached by pupils, and their rate of development, in order to facilitate learning' [45].

Differentiation:

Learning within drama needs to be differentiated, but how is this best done? It is particularly appropriate to think of differentiation in drama as a process not as a single event. This process involves recognising the variety of individual needs within a class, planning to meet those needs, considering appropriate delivery and then evaluating how effective these have been in allowing individuals to achieve. Pupils' outcomes will vary and in drama it is often the way the teacher responds to these outcomes that allows differentiation to take place because of the way practitioners give differentiated support and access to resources to the task.

For example, if the practitioner is in role as the hunter in 'Dirty Clothes' interacting with a small group who have taken on the role of the people of the mountains, she will listen carefully (diagnostically) to the level of response certain individuals are giving to her initial intervention. Within the dialogue she can then press some in terms of ideas and language e.g. "You have lost all vestiges of dignity. Only the animals retain their spirit. Say this is not so." Whilst she may have to encourage others who appear to need concrete questions to answer e.g. "When was the last time you did anything our people would be proud of?" The skill to diagnose and then respond instantly is at the heart of process drama work.

Examinations:

'Examinations are highly structured instruments of assessment which are intended to test specific knowledge and abilities at particular points in pupils' development' [46].

Examinations, tests and formal assessments are often used to rate pupils according to a comparative scale of achievement. It is helpful when looking at the various methods of doing this to be aware of the over-all system they belong in. The two most common assessment and testing methods are given below.

1 Norm-referencing.

An assessment system in which pupils are placed in rank order and pre-determined proportions are placed in the various grades. It implies that the grade given to a particular pupil depends upon a comparison between that pupil's performance and those of all the other pupils in the group rather than upon the absolute quality of the performance [47].

This gives rise to the normative curve which philosophically does not sit easily with drama education practice of focusing on the ability of all pupils to succeed and achieve. By definition a norm-referenced system will condemn the majority to mediocrity and automatically label a minority as failures.

2 Criterion referencing.

An assessment system in which an award or grade is made on the basis of the quality of the performance of a pupil irrespective of the performance of other pupils: this implies that teachers and pupils be given clear descriptions of the performance being sought [48].

Competency based procedures follow this method but again this does not sit too easily with drama education philosophy. This is because aims and learning outcomes in drama are invariably modified as the work progresses. Tying a course or series of lessons too closely to pre-specified learning outcomes can militate against the drama process and creativity itself. It could be argued that good practice in drama involves following hunches rather than sticking mechanistically to set plans. If this were accepted, then it would seem sensible that we should consider it a priority to give students skills in monitoring their own and their peers' work. This means that they will have to be aware of the agreed criteria for assessment and be able to contribute to the monitoring of their own progress.

Where can Drama be Assessed in the Curriculum?

Drama operates and can be inspected under many headings within the UK 5-16 curriculum. Six are readily identifiable:

- as a subject in its own right
- as a central component of the English National Curriculum
- alongside other Arts
- as a method of learning in other subjects
- as a contributor to cultural and social experience
- as a contributor to pupils' moral and spiritual development.

In UK primary schools, where drama is taught at all, it is often used as a learning medium contributing not just to English but a range of other subjects and dimensions of the curriculum. In some secondary schools the drama department is a department in its own right and not connected at all with the English department. In others it is closely tied in with the English Department, in others it operates within a creative or expressive arts department or faculty. Methods of assessment and evaluation are self-devised and are tied directly into schemes of work and the school's own assessment record keeping system.

From the beginning of the century until the present day the policy on drama and its assessment and evaluation appears to have been, 'Let many flowers bloom'. Drama practitioners have accepted no single over-arching conceptual framework. Nor is there a national framework in place. There are, however, many examples of excellent frameworks that have been developed in particular school contexts and which do a good job in creating dialogue between students and teachers and ensure development and progression.

Realistic Methods of Assessment and Evaluation

Many drama teachers have developed their own successful assessment and evaluation procedures. They know that pupils and they themselves need information on each other's achievements if their work is to progress. They are successful in that they give pupils and teachers information on each other's activities and perceptions of their work together. They provide a basis for informed description and intelligent judgment as a natural part of drama education activity. Often they contain a mixture of drama skills and knowledge, social and personal skills and wider learning areas. 'The spirit and style' of the work is reflected in the methods of assessment and evaluation.

It is unrealistic to expect any drama teacher to assess every child in each class every lesson. Many secondary teachers in the UK will teach up to 400 pupils a week. How could they possibly see each on an individual basis to give feedback? Yet this is what will help ensure progress. Methods are available to make the task achievable and realistically manageable. The emphasis has been on using a wide range of assessment tasks rather than relying on one only. This also means that different aspects of the drama process can be assessed in different ways, depending on what the activity is and the type of information being sought.

For example many teachers let their pupils keep a drama diary in which their individual response to work can be documented in written or visual form. These can also be used within the drama context e.g. writing in role. The diaries can then be used as a point of contact between pupil and teacher.

At regular intervals they also pick 4/5 pupils per lesson and assess their progress as the pupils are working. A quick word at the close of the lesson with these can help focus future development. The class need not know whom the teacher is assessing, so it also becomes a sort of motivational game if the formative nature of the process is stressed. During each scheme of work teacher and pupil will at some point write their own progress report in longhand in the diary or increasingly on a computer file.

The next section contains a variety of such examples of methods of assessment and evaluation in drama which have been developed in particular local education authority and school contexts [49]. They are not offered simply as blueprints or as definitive examples of good practice. They are offered as models, which have proved useful to teachers and groups of teachers in specific contexts. One thing is certain, the students who use them respond to what the particular assessment system values most. As you read through them you will see that they say a great deal about the practice and philosophy of drama teaching in that particular institution, authority or school context. All methods of assessment and evaluation have strengths and weaknesses and to emphasise this, a brief comment is given on the 'Up-side' and 'Down-side' of each of the examples.

Examples of Assessment and Evaluation Methods and Record Keeping Systems in Drama

Example 1
Drama Statement Bank Directory (page 104)

Statements refer to possible achievements and in this example each of these have 4 levels of grade related criteria. Ten statements have been chosen to suggest the type of statement that could be used.

Up-side: The practitioner and/or student can choose whatever statements they feel are appropriate in their context and stage of development. These could be stored on computer and selected to generate a response or report. The possibility exists within this format to negotiate and set future targets. The form can be filled in quickly.

Down-side: A quick visual survey of progress cannot be made without comparing all previous forms. This could perhaps be addressed by adding more right hand page columns and additional comment space for 5/6 terms/projects.

Example 2
Drama Diary (page 106)

The diary is principally the responsibility of the student who will have it with him at every session. There is usually a 'review' of work at a set period, perhaps once a term or half term by the practitioner and student. In taking in the drama diaries the teacher can look at the evidence in the diary for development.

Up-side: The diary can also be used to build belief in a drama e.g. writing a letter in role that informs the next stage of the work. Entries can be drawn and photographs can be put in. In this sense the diary is not just a 'we did this today'. It is a more pro-active document that allows the concepts and ideas to be worked on outside the official drama time. The practitioner can also enter into a short dialogue with the student that allows progress to be monitored through the writing/drawings/graphs of involvement and photographs produced in response to the drama.

Down-side: Drama diaries are heavy! They can take up a lot of time as the practitioner needs to respond in writing if the student is to feel that work is being valued. There also needs to be a clear understanding between the practitioner and student that the diaries will be used for formative and summative purposes. In the reviews there can be a tendency to fall into description. One possibility used by some practitioners is to offer a range of twenty points for the students to choose five at a time from and then comment on.

Example 3
Drama Self-Assessment Forms and Records of Achievement (page 107)

Drama self-assessment forms can be built up into a record of achievement. Records of achievement, in various formats, are used by many drama departments at secondary school level. The drama-specific records sometimes have to fit in with a pre-determined agreed school format. At other times the Head of Drama has complete freedom. This is a record of one eleven year old pupil's work over three projects (one each term) and his final drama project self-assessment form which relates to the whole year's work.

Up-side: The practitioner only has to 'sign off' the pupil's consideration and record of his progress although there is a space for any other comments if needed. The drama and social skills considered in each project are re-stated and reinforced on each form. The pupil has ownership of the method of recording and there is some scope for negotiation about perceptions of progress and targets. In this case all the forms were kept in a filing cabinet in the drama studio to which pupils had access by request.

Down-side: Progress cannot be monitored quickly at a glance without reading back through previous project forms. There is no space for the practitioner to put her perceptions in the 'Always/Sometimes/Never columns' on the final drama self-assessment form. Challenge of these has to be through 'Any other comments'. There is no direct link between comments and the drama and social skills listed for each project.

Example 4
Record of Achievement (page 110)

This example from a secondary school comprises one record of achievement in the upper school and another in the lower school. The upper school method involves a tick system with grade-related criteria for both cross-curricular and drama-specific skills, knowledge and understanding. In the lower school by contrast the individual is asked to comment in longhand on the achievement of specific learning outcomes. Within one year the individual would complete three or four of these specifically focused learning profiles.

Up-side: The lower school form encourages a dialogue between pupil and teacher about what has been taught and learnt. The upper school form allows a comprehensive summative statement of student progress to be made by the teacher and commented on by the student.

Down-side: The methods of assessment are not consistent across the school in that the onus falls on the pupil in the Lower School and the teacher in the Upper School. The teacher has a heavy commitment in terms of time in both these methods of assessment. Scope for pupil input on the upper school form is limited, unless of course the grades are negotiated

Example 5
Curriculum Maps (page 112)

This assessment and evaluation method is based upon a series of curriculum maps and is used within an Expressive Arts Department. The students negotiate their way through the year with the guidance of these maps. At the end of their journey through each 'mapped module' the teacher spends a double session negotiating what will be written on the form. First of all each pupil gives herself a grade from 1/2/3/4. and sets her targets for future work in the light of this communication and negotiation. Two module examples are given here to allow for comparison.

Up-side: The emphasis on this method as a formative process is strong as implied in statements such as "This is not a test' and 'My grade'. Generic skills are emphasised by remaining constant on the Module Forms whilst specific processes and techniques change. The relationship between skills, processes and techniques is clearly identified in this way. The regularity of the procedure can encourage the students themselves to become reflective practitioners.

Down-side: This grading is based entirely on 'feeling response', there are no objective criteria and it is thus totally subjective. The only guidance given is that 3 represents 'average' attainment. If this procedure took place every 8 weeks the block time taken for such protracted negotiation could be problematic and over-heavy. One method to spread this load would be to target 4/5 students every week over 8 weeks and to give them direct feedback immediately for just a few minutes after the session. The form would then provide a 'snapshot' of progress and could be added to briefly in the final week but in a much shorter time scale.

Example 6
Drama Policy Statement (page 114)

This extract from a Drama Policy Statement outlines one high school's whole approach to assessment and evaluation. The document is targeted at students and their parents and moves from a general statement of purpose, through a series of selected drama attainment targets to drama profiles. The member of staff in charge of drama within this English department did what in reality often happens, which is to take what had worked in one situation (his old school) and adapt the most relevant parts to another. He also realised that assessment and evaluation methods need to be placed within a whole Drama Policy Statement. This is of course true of all the previous examples which have in this sense been given 'out of context'. We finish this section by intentionally placing the final example in the context it would usually be found in schools in the UK. We will leave you to work out the 'Up-sides' and 'Down-sides' of the methods employed!

Example 1

Name _____ Date _____ Term/Project _____

Please tick the level (1 or 2 or 3 or 4) which you feel you achieved overall in the last term/project.
S= student   P= practitioner

[1] Role in drama (1, 2, 3, 4 & 5)

[1] *Suspend disbelief:*   S   P
    [1]   Cannot suspend disbelief save by accident/chance
    [2]   Some attempt to suspend disbelief but cannot sustain
    [3]   Can suspend and sustain disbelief at a consistent level
    [4]   Can suspend and sustain disbelief with a high level of commitment

[2] *Can adopt a role:*   S   P
    [1]   Cannot adopt a role save by accident/chance
    [2]   Some attempt to adopt a role but cannot sustain it
    [3]   Can adopt and sustain a role
    [4]   Can adopt, sustain and develop a role

[3] *Can verbalise in role:*   S   P
    [1]   Cannot verbalise in role save by accident/chance
    [2]   Some attempt to verbalise in role but cannot sustain
    [3]   Can verbalise competently in role
    [4]   Can verbalise to an effective and accomplished level

[4] *Can use body language (in role):*   S   P
    [1]   Cannot use body language save by accident/chance
    [2]   Some awareness and attempt to use body language
    [3]   Can use body language competently
    [4]   Can use body language to an effective and accomplished level

[5] *Can interact and negotiate [in role]:*   S   P
    [1]   Cannot interact in role save by accident/chance
    [2]   Some attempt to interact in role
    [3]   Can interact consistently in role with some attempt at negotiation
    [4]   Can interact and negotiate in role to an effective and accomplished level

[2] Use of drama forms and elements (6, 7, 8, 9 & 10)

[6] *Can use imaginative space:*   S   P
    [1]   Cannot use imaginative space save by accident/chance
    [2]   Some awareness of and attempt to use imaginative space
    [3]   Competent use of imaginative space
    [4]   Effective and accomplished use of imaginative space

[7] *Can devise appropriate drama form*   S   P

    [1]   Is not aware of different drama forms/cannot devise appropriate forms; uses only by chance

    [2]   Some awareness of, and attempt to develop, appropriate drama forms

    [3]   Competent use of appropriate drama forms

    [4]   Can use and develop appropriate drama forms

[8] *Can recognise and use main drama elements: (Focus, tension, symbol, metaphor, contrast etc.]*   S   P

    [1]   Cannot recognise main drama elements; use only by chance

    [2]   Some recognition of main drama elements

    [3]   Competent use of main drama elements

    [4]   Accomplished use and development of main drama elements

[9] *Can use basic drama resources:*   S   P

    [1]   Shows no awareness of the use of drama resources save by chance

    [2]   Shows some awareness and use of drama resources

    [3]   Competent use of drama resources

    [4]   Accomplished and effective use of resources

[10] *Can reflect upon and analyse the implications/quality of drama work undertaken*   S   P

    [1]   Cannot recognise implications and quality save by chance

    [2]   Shows some awareness of implications and quality of drama work undertaken

    [3]   Can recognise implications and quality and articulate views on drama work undertaken

    [4]   Articulate recognition of the implications and quality of drama work undertaken which is then acted upon i.e. can discuss how future developments will be affected by present expression.

Student - *The thing I do best/ Any other comments:*

My target for the next term/project:

Practitioner - *Any other comments:*

Signed _____ Student _____

Practitioner_____ Date _____

Example 2

Name: Holly Rotherham   Date: _____

Review of the term's work: Autumn Term A

> The thing I enjoyed the most in this half term was the hostage drama about a landlord that owed money but couldn't repay a loan and his family were taken hostage. I played the daughter and was the one who came up with the idea of flashing the light which was what got us rescued in the end . I wrote the note that was never found and it is on the first page of my diary. I think it shows how scared they all really were and how none of them ever thought this could happen in the middle of the day.
>
> My favourite game we played was the card game. I enjoyed my first half term of drama and I hope to enjoy the rest of the course just as much..

Target to carry forward
(What do I need to do next?)

> 1. To be able to sustain and develop my future characters
>
> 2. To be more outgoing while in role

Teacher Comment:

> *I'm glad you've enjoyed the course so far Holly, and I can see that you are still feeling your way in! You have obviously thought carefully about what you want from the course. Well done!*

Teacher Signature: _____   Date: _____

_____

Example 3

Name: *Gavin Travers* Form: *7W*

Project Title: *Project 1 Black & White Movie*

DRAMA SKILLS:	SOCIAL SKILLS:	GROUP SIZE:
Play-in-role	Communication	4 - 5
Still image	Compromising	
Miming	Mixed Groups	
Freeze Frame	Listening	
Interactive		
Narrator		

What was your favourite part of this project?

The rides at the start of the exhibition was the best part of the project for me.

What was your least favourite part of this project?

I do not have a least favourite part of this project as I enjoyed it all.

If you were going to do this project again how would you improve it?

I would improve my project by coming up with better ideas.

What do you need to work on in the next project?

I need to work on my communications skills.

Teacher _____ Pupil _____ Date _____

Any other comments:

_____

Name: *Gavin Travers* Form: *7W*

Project Title: *Project 2 Amazing Maze*

DRAMA SKILLS:	SOCIAL SKILLS:	GROUP SIZE:
Still-image	Work with new people	Small Group
Imagination	Imagination	Big Group
Map-making	Co-operation in a big group	
Working in role	Confidence	
Mantle-of-the-expert	Fair Play	

What was your favourite part of this project?

My favourite part of this project was showing our work to the King (Miss Crawley) because I had to do all the talking and become a bit swotty.

What was your least favourite part of this project?

My least favourite part of this project was designing the maze because it took a long time to get the maze right.

If you were going to do this project again how would you improve it?

I would definitely make the presentation of the maze neater because the maze was a little scruffy.

What do you need to work on in the next project?

I think I need to work on my presentation and my co-operation because I seem to take over on everything.

Teacher _____ Pupil _____ Date _____

Any other comments:

_____

Name: __Gavin Travers_____ Form: __7W_____

Project Title: __Project 3 Space Mission_____

DRAMA SKILLS:	SOCIAL SKILLS:	GROUP SIZE:
Mantle-of-the-expert	Co-operation	Individual
Still image	Belief	Small Group
Working in role	Imagination	Big Group
Guided Fantasy	Communication	
Confidence		
Working with people		

What was your favourite part of this project?

My favourite part of this project was the big debate on whether to take the alien (Miss Crawley) or not because I enjoyed the reasoning.

What was your least favourite part of this project?

I didn't like building the space-craft because I thought it took too long to build and dismantle.

If you were going to do this project again how would you improve it?

I think I did really well in this project but I would improve the presentation of my work.

What do you need to work on in the next project?

I think the only thing I need to work on is my presentation, as I think I have let the people in my group do more which was my last target.

Teacher _____ Pupil _____ Date _____

Any other comments:

_____

Drama self-assessment form

Year 7

Name: *Gavin Travers* _____ Form **7W** Date _____

Please answer these questions:

	Always	Sometimes	Never
1. Working with others:			
Am I willing to work with everyone in the group?		✔	
Do I always work with the same people?	✔		
Do I help other people to get involved in the work?	✔		
Can I disagree with people without quarrelling?		✔	
Any other comment:			
2. Discussion:			
Do I contribute ideas to the group?	✔		
Do I develop other people's ideas?		✔	
Can I listen?	✔		
Can I criticise in a constructive and helpful way?		✔	
Any other comment:			
3. Working in role:			
Am I willing to adopt a variety of roles?		✔	
Do I sustain and deepen the roles I adopt?		✔	
Do I respond to what other people are doing in the drama?	✔		
Can I opt out without spoiling it for other people?		✔	
Any other comment:			
4. Thinking about drama:			
Can I take criticism and advice?	✔		
Can I discuss my own weaknesses?		✔	
Do I ask the teacher when I don't understand or am confused?	✔		
Any other comment:			

Thinking about my own learning

My most important contribution to the work of the group this year has been:

My idea about flying out of the back of the ambulance in the silent movies.

My reasons for choosing this aspect of my work are as follows:

1. *It slotted in with our movie.*
2. *It looked funny.*
3. *It was good fun to act.*

I would like to improve my drama in the following way:

In silent, black and white movies I shouldn't make a sound, but I tend to do an over-the-top silly scream. I do not take over everything and my ideas are good but I need to work on my presentation.

Teacher _____ Pupil _____ Date _____

Any other comments: _____

Example 4

Upper School Drama

Name

Form   Date

Level:
A   Has thorough mastery of these skills
B   Uses these skills with confidence
C   Manages to use and apply these skills
D   Is aware of the skills required
E   Has had experience in this area

Cross Curricular Skills:
Communication
Numeracy
Reference
Problem solving
Dexterity
Graphicacy
Creativity
Organisation

Subject Assessment

This pupil has	A	B	C	D	E
1. Shown commitment to the work					
2. Assumed role					
3. [a] suspended } disbelief					
[b] sustained } the pretend situation					
4. Employed language appropriate to the role/task					
5. Reacted to the focal point of the drama					
6. Within the group:					
[a] co-operated					
[b] listened to others					
[c] shared ideas					
[d] planned democratically					
7. Evaluated the work					
Reflected upon the work					
8. Shown understanding of theatrical terms and related topics					

Teacher Comment (if required)

Signed: _____

Example 4 *continued*

Lower School Drama

Name _____ From _____

Length of course _____ Date _____

During this part of the course you will cover work on:
1   Introductory exercises
2   Role play - individual, small and whole group work

What you will be required to do is:
   a. After a series of lessons think about what you have done - did you make a great effort to be involved? Could you have worked harder? Do you need to improve next time?
   b. You will need to write down, in a few sentences, your feelings about what you have achieved. You will be given time for this at the end of the series of lessons. We will sometimes have discussed these during or at the end of the lessons.

Individual / Small / Whole Group Role Play

During the role play on_____ I was looking at your ability to:

1. Take on a role imaginatively and be committed to it

   Your comment: _____

   _____

   My comment: _____

   _____

2. Be part of the pretend and keep it going

   Your comment: _____

   _____

   My comment: _____

   _____

3. Use the language needed for that role

   Your comment: _____

   _____

   My comment _____

   _____

Example 5

Be honest and truthful - this is not a test:
Write down briefly   [a] what you found easy or difficult in the module;
  [b] what you enjoyed or didn't enjoy and WHY
  [c] did you do your best or could you have done better, and WHY
  [d] was there anything else which affected your progress?

Consider all these and give yourself a grade

Module 3 : "City" Date _____ to _____		
	ATTENDANCE	☐
Processes; techniques; materials/equipment; turning into colour; colour/place associations; use of gels to create mood; texture and associations with people (e.g. abrasive); spatial awareness; colour and sound to create multi-media presentation. Tutor comments Signed:_____ Date:_____	Workshop behaviour Participation/involvement Reliability/independence Response to advice/instruction Level of understanding Generation of ideas Quality of preparation work Handling of equipment/ materials Control of techniques Quality of end product Home course work R.O.A. Nos.	
Pupil Comments MY GRADE ☐ Signed: _____		

Example 5 *continued*

Module 3 : "World"	Date _____ to _____
	ATTENDANCE [ ]

Processes; techniques; materials/equipment; understanding and interpreting non-verbal responses development of language flow, communication skills - how to challenge, discuss persuade, present and justify a point of view; multi-cultural presentation; using travel info and workshop on Ethnic Dance. Tutor comments Signed:_____ Date: _____	Workshop behaviour Participation/involvement Reliability/independence Response to advice/instruction Level of understanding Generation of ideas Quality of preparation work Handling of equipment/materials Control of techniques Quality of end product Home course work R.O.A. Nos.

Pupil comments

Targets for the future

MY GRADE [ ]   Signed: _____

Example 6

Drama Policy Statement
Monitoring, Assessment, Recording, Reporting and Accountability

Purpose

Monitoring, assessment, recording, reporting and accountability (MARRA) are central to the development of students' learning and are used to diagnose, monitor, evaluate and celebrate students' progress and recognise their achievements. They are used to motivate and enhance student learning, to collect evidence of progress and achievements and to inform students, staff and parents. These processes help to evaluate learning and teaching strategies to inform planning for future learning.

Broad Guidelines
General

Assessment refers to formal assessment, not everyday marking.
The whole curriculum encompasses a variety of experiences of learning and development, some of which are not assessable. 'In drama in education, one is attempting to assess an inner experience and not merely the external manifestations of that experience'. *(O'Neil,C. Lambert,A. Linnel,R. Warr-Wood, J.1981 Drama Guidelines Heinemann)*

Drama will be commonly broken down into PLANNING and Realisation (Making) and EVALUATION (Appraising) of one's own work and that of others. *(As recommended by The Arts in School Project 1990 Arts Council)*. Drama will also be used to assess AT1 English.

Assessment

- The Drama Curriculum will be divided into sections (consisting of core experiences) with defined objectives and assessment criteria.
- Assessment (unlike marking) will not be recorded in terms of an attainment level.
- Assessment in Drama will be on-going. A variety of different forms of assessment e.g. written, oral, photographs, audio/visual recordings, practical, will be built into drama time so that students and teacher can assess the drama in progress.
- Reflection on the work will act as a vehicle for learning and creating meanings. The teacher will adopt the role of 'structural agent' but the students will have their say and consequently take ownership of the drama. Thus they will take responsibility for their learning.
- Outside 'drama time' assessment will take place, particularly with older students. Dramatic form will be discussed, analysed and appreciated. Personal connections might be made and points of view shared.

Recording

- Students will record achievement on a Drama profile at least once per term.
- Teachers will review work and assessments with individual students.
- Teachers will make overall assessments of progress, attainment and effort twice per year, which will be recorded on the Central Record System.

Reporting to parents

- During an academic year there will be a pastoral parents' evening, an interim report, a parents' evening and a full report.
- The timing of these reports will be reviewed annually in Council.
- Interim reports will contain a progress and effort grade and a student personal statement at Key Stage 3.
- All attainment grades will be given at Key Stage 4 and comments will contain staff statements on perceived strengths and weaknesses and targets for future developments.

Reporting to others

All reporting, even if verbal in the first instance, should have a written element for student records.

Implementation and Monitoring

1. All deadlines for completion of subject teacher, group tutor and student pages for reports will be published in the annual calendar before the end of the previous academic year.

2. On end-of-year reports, name boxes must contain the proper forename and surname but other names can be used in comments. Staff comments must contain information on strengths, weaknesses and target(s) for improvement/progress. Where an exam has been set, the result must be recorded as a percentage or as a GCSE grade, as appropriate.

3. Dates for parents' evenings and reviews will be published in the calendar together with dates for sending reports home.

4. The Drama team will review the policy annually at a July meeting.

5. Differentiating between effort and progress grades needs to be continually explained and reinforced to students by Drama staff.

Assessment criteria

Attainment Targets at KS3

At KS3 Drama will be assessed following two attainment targets:

Attainment Target 1
Investigating (Planning) and Realisation (Making).
The development of the ability to generate and shape dramatic forms in order to explore and express ideas.

Attainment Target 2
Performing and Evaluation (Appraising).
The development of the ability to engage and communicate with an audience in a dramatic presentation, and the ability to express understanding, discernment and appreciation of Drama in all its forms.

The following criteria should be assessed when evaluating students' practical work:

> Workshop behaviour
> Participation/Involvement
> Reliability/Independence
> Response to advice/Instruction
> Level of understanding
> Generation of ideas
> Quality of preparation work
> Handling of equipment/materials
> Control of techniques/Drama conventions
> Quality of 'end product'

A comment on one or more of these will be recorded on student record cards for Drama, along with an overall effort grade, for the lesson targeted.

These criteria will also be assessed on Drama Profile sheets, each being given an effort grade for the student. It is hoped that eventually pupils will complete a Drama Profile at the end of every Core Experience (Module) for Drama.

The development of such Core Experiences is, at present, an ongoing process.

Drama Profile

Name	Form

Module Titles

Teacher Comments	Assessment Criteria	Effort
	Workshop behaviour	
	Participation/Involvement	
	Response to instructions	
	Understanding of techniques & Drama conventions	
	Level of co-operation & teamwork	
Signed Date	Generation of ideas	
_____ _____	Use of equipment/materials	

Pupil Comments

Targets

Signed _____ Date _____

Drama Profile

Name	Form
Module Titles	

Parent's Comments

Signed _____ Date _____

_____   _____

Mapping a Drama Curriculum

Good practice in drama education, assessment and evaluation celebrates achievement, allows the individual to make active ongoing contributions to the measurement of progress, clearly outlines responsibilities and does so in a language that is accessible to all. It liberates insights rather than restricting developments.

However there are still some questions that are difficult to answer and are being asked by practitioners [50]. For example, can an account of progress in drama satisfactory to all practitioners be devised? If 'getting better' at drama does not simply mean getting better at acting could it be said to mean that a person can take an idea and translate it into dramatic form or does it also mean that they become 'a better person' as well? How can we ensure that individuals get a fair assessment and are given the same grades regardless of who is assessing? Does focusing on ability in drama shift attention away from developments and learning which occur as a result of the drama? Do attempts to teach skills and isolate ability in drama from learning through drama lead to low ceilings of achievement? Are the most important things in drama impossible to assess?

The content of the curriculum is still flexible in drama, but should it be? How can this be squared with the development of a national framework for progression and achievement in drama? Does there need to be such a thing when drama is flourishing anyway? To deliver content, resources and tasks have to be designed and created to enable students to acquire knowledge and understanding as well as developing drama skills. Whilst working on the task, members of the group have the support to help and guide them through the process and the teacher has control over differentiation by resource, task, support and response to outcome. Is this enough?

There are many threats and opportunities that face practitioners when grappling with such issues which are at the heart of drama education work. For example, one identified form of drama could become dominant and so determine and thereby restrict content and methodologies used by others. The teaching of drama and theatre skills in the traditional sense could assume priority over the teaching and learning of personal and social skills or vice versa. The need for schools to have an overall drama policy related to their catchment area and ability range is championed by some and derided by others. The business of assessing skills may take precedence over the process of evaluating engagement. The business of assessment could distort the nature of the drama work. An attempt at a prescriptive definition of progress, in terms of content only, could result in a distorted and over-simplified account. The language used to assess and evaluate could become so complex that it alienates the very people it is meant to be of use to.

Assessment and Evaluation -A & E- if kept in place can be very useful servants to all those engaged in drama education. If they are allowed to become the masters, the pressure on all those involved can have serious effects not just on the quality of work but the health of all participants. A & E in drama should never be allowed to come to stand for Accident & Emergency! John Ruskin the nineteenth century philosopher, suggested that there were three important rules to follow about work and they seem particularly appropriate to the issue of assessment and evaluation and the pressure of inspection in drama:

'... be fit for it... do not do too much of it... have a sense of success in it.' *

Good Luck!

REFERENCES

1 Westacott, H.D. 1980 *The Walkers Handbook* Penguin

2 For a fuller discussion and definition of Pretexts see O'Neil, C. 1995 Heinemann USA *Drama Worlds* and Owens, A. & Barber, K. 1987 *Dramaworks* Carel Press

3 *The Fight for Drama The Fight for Education*. A conference held by the National Association of Teachers of Drama at Birmingham Polytechnic in 1989

4 *'The Way West'* in O'Neil,C. & Lambert, A. 1984 *Drama Structures* Hutchinson

5 Teeakialio in Barker, C. l980 *Theatre Games* Methuen

6 O'Toole, J. 1992 *The Process of Drama* Routledge

7 'Attitude in action', a phrase coined by Dorothy Heathcote, discussed in Wagner, B.J. 1979 *Dorothy Heathcote, Drama as a Learning Medium* p.68 For further developments in this discussion see Bolton, G. 1998 *Acting in Classroom Drama* Trentham Books

8 For a fuller discussion of role see: Winston, J. & Tandy, M. 1998 *Beginning Drama 4-11* David Fulton Ltd. p.38, O'Toole, J 1992 *The Process of Drama* Routledge p.68-69, Neelands, 1990 *Structuring Drama Work* CUP p.32-33, Fleming, 1997, *The Art of Drama Teaching* David Fulton Ltd p.62, Wooland, B. 1993 *The Teaching of Drama in the Primary School,* Longman p.35-36, Morgan, N. & Saxton, J. 1987 *Teaching Drama* Hutchinson p.38, O'Neil, C.1995 *Drama Worlds* Heinemann USA p. 69-91

9 For a full discussion of Signing see Aston, E. & Savona, G. 1991 *Theatre as a Sign System* Routledge

10 Lawrence, C. 1982 *'Teacher in Role'* 2D

11 Practical session run by Guy Williams and Martin Bell

12 Boal, A. 1995 *The Rainbow of Desire* Routledge Chpt. 3 The Aesthetic Space, Friere, P. 1996 *Letters to Christina* Routledge - The Educational Space

13 In Witkin, R. 1974 *The Intelligence of Feeling* Heinemann

14 John Rainer running a workshop for the Cheshire Association for Drama Education 1996

15 O'Neill, C. 1995 *Drama Worlds* Heinemann USA xi, Fleming M. 1994 *Starting Drama Teaching* David Fulton Ltd.

16 Greenwood, C. 1996 *Breaking the Cycle of Violence. A case Study of Blah, Blah, Blah's Romeo and Juliet'* SCYPT Journal

17 For a full discussion of conventions see Neelands, J. 1989 *Structuring Drama Work* CUP

18 Jonothan Neelands teaching on the Advanced Diploma in Drama Education course run by Cheshire LEA and Chester College 1988 at the Malpas Centre, Cheshire.

19 Social Health in: Wagner, B.J. 1979 *Dorothy Heathcote: Drama as a Learning Medium,* O'Toole, J. 1992 The Process of Drama Routledge p.117-119

20 Wolfensburger, W. & Thomas, S. 1983 PASSING- *A method of evaluating the quality of human services according to the principle-Normalization Criteria and Ratings Manual* 2nd Edition. Canadian National Institute on Mental Retardation Publ.

21 Vincent, J. & Peaker, A. 1990 *The Arts in Prisons Towards a Sense of Achievement* CRSP Loughbrough University Publ.

22 Devised with Mary Gillot and Anita Birkbeck Based on the book by James, S.1990 *My Friend Whale* Walker Books

23 Turner,V. 1982 *From Ritual to Theatre: The Human Seriousness of Play* PAJ Publ.

24 Boal, A. 1979 *Theatre of the Oppressed* Pluto Press

25 Zeichener ,K.M.& Liston, D.P. 1990 *Traditions of reform in US Teacher Education: Journal of Teacher Education,* 41(2)3-20

26 Fleming, M. 1997 *The Art of Drama Teaching* David Fulton Ltd

27 Hornbrook, D.1989 *Education in Drama: Casting the Dramatic Curriculum* David Fulton Press

28 *Report of the Task Group on Assessment and Testing* 1987 HMSO

29 Eisner, E. in Calouste Gulbenkian Foundation Advisory Committee 1982 *The Arts in Schools* CGF

30 Toole, J. 1995 Speaking at the World Congress of IDEA Brisbane, Australia

31 *DFEE/QCA 1999 The National Curriculum Handbook for Secondary Teachers* DFEE/QCA Publ.

32 Hornbrook, 1991 p.136

33 Freeman, J. 1997 *Performance Practice Vol.2* Chester College Publ.

34 Macnamara, J. in *All Our Futures: Creativity, Culture and Education* 1999 National Advisory Committee on Creative and Cultural Education DFEE

35 HMI *Drama 5-16 Curriculum Matters* No 17 HMSO

36 John Hertrich HMI Speaking at the North West Drama Conference, Manchester Metropolitan University 1999

37 Secondary Heads Association 1999 *Drama Sets You Free* SHA Publ.

38 DES *Education Reform Act* 1988 HMSO

39 *Report of the Task Group on Assessment and Testing* 1987 HMSO

40 Section 1, Point 2

41 Section 1, Point 2

42 Calouste Gulbenkian Foundation Advisory Committee 1982 *The Arts in Schools* CGF

43 Eisner, E. in Calouste Gulbenkian Foundation Advisory Committee 1982 *The Arts in Schools* CGF

44 TGAT para 40

45 Ibid para 40

46 Calouste Gulbenkian Foundation Advisory Committee 1982 *The Arts in Schools* CGF

47 *Report of the Task Group on Assessment and Testing* 1987 HMSO Preface And Glossary

48 Ibid

49 The authors would like to thank the drama staff of the many schools that contributed to the development of the methods of assessment, especially:
- Victoria High School, Crewe
- Great Sankey High, Warrington
- Malbank School and Sixth Form Centre
- Stanney High School, Ellesmere Port
- Sutton High School, Ellesmere Port
- Kingsway High School, Chester

50 See for detailed discussion of these issues Fleming, M. *Starting Drama Teaching* 1994 Chapter 9 and Morgan, N. & Saxton, J. 1998 NADIE Journal.

DRAMA EDUCATION ASSOCIATIONS, ORGANISATIONS & PUBLICATIONS

Publications only are marked with a*

All other entries are associations and organisations which also produce publications, often from conferences and courses they run.

Centre for Studies in Drama in Education,
Faculty of Education, University of Central England in Birmingham, Westbourne Road, Edgbaston, Birmingham, B15 3TN.

Dorothy Heathcote Archive* - Manchester Metropolitan University, Didsbury School of Education, Manchester

Dorothy Heathcote Catalogue* - Audio Visual Centre, University of Newcastle, The Medical School, Framlington Place, Newcastle upon Tyne, NE2 4HH.

International Drama Education Researchers Network,
School of Education, University of Exeter, Exeter, Devon, EX1 2LU.

Theatre in Prisons and Probation Centre, Manchester University Drama Dept, Oxford Road, Manchester, M14 6HD.

Local Drama Associations - there are many local associations throughout the UK which provide valuable support networks. For example: **Cheshire Association for Drama Education, (CADE),** Cheshire Drama Resource Centre, Verdin Centre, High Street, Winsford, Cheshire, CW7 2AY

National Drama, at Central School of Speech and Drama, Eton Avenue, London, NW33Hy
National Association of Teachers of Drama, Gillian Adamson, 118 Moreton Road, Bushbury, Wolverhampton, WV108LB

National Association for Drama in Education Australia, PO Box 163, Albert Street, Brisbane, Queensland 4002 Australia.

New Theatre Quarterly,* The Edinburgh Building, Shaftesbury Road, Cambridge, CB2 2RU.

Research in Drama Education,* Carfax Publishing Company, P.O. Box 25, Abingdon, Oxfordshire, OX14 3UE.

ILLUSTRATIVE BOOKLIST

If you are interested in reading more about Drama Education

In Primary Schools

Bolton, G. 1991 *New Perspectives on Classroom Drama,* Simon & Schuster
Clipson-Boyles, S. 1998 *Drama in Primary English Teaching* David Fulton Publ.
Davies, G. 1983 *Practical Primary Drama,* Heinemann
Griffiths, D. 1991 *An Early Start to Drama,* Simon & Schuster
Heathcote, D. & Bolton, G. 1995 *Drama for Learning: An Account of Dorothy Heathcote's Mantle of the Expert,* USA Heinemann
Readman, G. Lamont, G. *Drama: A Handbook for Primary Teachers,* 1994 BBC Books
Winston, J. & Tandy, M. 1998 *Begining Drama 4-11* David Fulton Publ.
Woolland, B. 1993 *The Teaching of Drama in the Primary School,* Longman

In Secondary Schools

Airs, J. & Ball, C. 1998 *Key Ideas in Drama* Folens Publ.
Barlow, S. & Skidmore, S. 1995 *Drama Form,* Hodder & Stoughton
Cooper, S. & Mackey, S. 1995 *An Approach for Advanced Level* Stanley Thornes
Flemming, M. 1994 *Starting Drama Teaching* David Fulton Publ.
Flemming, M. 1998 *The Art of Drama Teaching* David Fulton Publ.
Kempe, A. 1998 *The GCSE Drama Course Book* 2nd Edition, Blackwell
Kempe, A. 1988 *The Drama Sampler,* Blackwell
Kempe, A. & Warner, L. 1997 *Starting With Scripts* Stanley Thornes

Morgan, N. & Saxton, J. (1987) *Teaching Drama,* Hutchinson
Nixon, J. 1987 *Teaching Drama,* Macmillan Educ.
Mackey, S. 1997 *Practical Theatre A post-16 approach* Stanley Thornes
Marston, P., Brockbank, K., McGuire, B., Morton, S. 1990 *Drama 14-16,* Stanley Thornes
McGuire, B. 1998 *Student Handbook for Drama* Pearson Publ.
Neelands, J. 1983 *Making Sense of Drama,* Heinemann
Neelands, J. 1990 *Structuring Drama Work,* C.U.P.
Neelands, J. 1992 *Learning Through Imagined Experience,* Hodder & Stoughton
Neelands, J. 1993 *Drama and I.T. The Human Dimension,* NATE & NCET
Neelands, J. 1998 *Begining Drama 11-14* David Fulton Publ.
O'Neill, C. & Lambert, A. 1984 *Drama Structures,* Hutchinson
O'Neill, C., Lambert, A., Linnel, R. & Warr-Wood, J. 1976 *Drama Guidelines,* Heinemann
O'Toole, J. & Haseman, B. 1987 *Drama Wise - An Introduction to GCSE,* Heinemann
Somers, J. 1994 *Drama in the Curriculum,* Cassell
Taylor, K. (Edit) 1991 *Drama Strategies,* Heinemann

Special Educational Needs

Kempe, A. (edit.) 1996 *Drama Education and Special Educational Needs* Stanley Thornes
Peter, M. 1994 *Drama for all,* David Fulton Publ.
Peter, M. 1994 *Making Drama Special,* David Fulton Publ.
Roberts, T. 1988 *Special Needs in Ordinary Schools - Arts in the Primary Curriculum,* Cassel

Boal, A. 1979 *Theatre of the Oppressed*, Pluto
Boal, A. 1992 *Games for Actors and Non-Actors*, Routledge
Boal, A. 1995 *The Rainbow of Desire*, Routledge
Cox, M. (Ed) 1992 *Shakespeare Comes to Broadmoor*, Jessica Kingsley Publ.
Crimmens, P. 1998 *Storymaking and Creative Groupwork with Older People* Jessica Kingsley
Jennings, S. 1987 *Dramatherapy Theory and Practice*, Jessica Kingsley Press
Jennings, S. 1992 *Dramatherapy Theory and Practice 2*, Jessica Kingsley Press
Jennings, S. 1993 *Introduction to Dramatherapy*, Jessica Kingsley Press
Jennings, S. 1994 *The Handbook of Dramatherapy*, Routledge
Johnson, L. & O'Neill, C. 1984 *Dorothy Heathcote: Collected Writings*, Hutchinson
Kershaw, B. 1992 *The Politics of Performance*, Routledge
Owens, A. & Barber, K. 1997 *Dramaworks* Carel Press
Thompson, J. 1998 *Prison Theatre* Jessica Kingsley
Tomlinson, R. 1982 *Disability, Theatre and Education*, Condor
Wagner, B.J. 1979 *Dorothy Heathcote - Drama as a Learning Medium*, Hutchinson
Theoretical Perspectives
Abbs, P. 1989 *The Symbolic Order*, The Falmer Press
Best, D. 1992 *The Rationality of Feeling: Understanding the Arts in Education*, The Falmer Press
Bolton, G. 1979 *Towards a Theory of Drama Education*, Longman

Bolton, G. 1984 *Drama as Education*, Longman
Bolton, G. 1998 *Acting in Classroom Drama* Trentham Books
Courtenay, R. 1974 *Play Drama and Thought*, Cassell
Courtenay, R. 1980 *The Dramatic Curriculum*, Heinemann
Davies, D. & Lawrence, C. 1986 *Gavin Bolton : Selected Writings*, Longman
Day, C. & Norman, J. 1983 *Issues in Educational Drama*, Falmer Press
Hargreaves, D. (Edit) 1989 *Children and the Arts*, O.U.P.
Hornbrook, D. 1989 *Education and Dramatic Art*, Blackwell Educ.
Hornbrook, D. 1991 *Education in Drama*, Falmer Press
Jackson, T. 1993 *Learning Through Theatre*, Routledge
McGregor, L. Tate, M. & Robinson, K. 1977 *Learning Through Drama*, Heinemann
National Advisory Committee on Creative and Cultural education 1999 *All Our Futures: Creativity, Culture and Education* DfEE
O'Neill, C. 1995 *Drama Worlds*, Heinemann USA
O'Toole, J. 1977 *Theatre in Education*, Hodder & Stoughton
O'Toole, J. 1992 *The Process of Drama*, Routledge
Ross, M. 1984 *The Development of Aesthetic Experience*, Pergammon
Robinson, K. 1980 *Exploring Theatre & Education*, Heinemann
Slade, P. 1954 *Child Drama*, Univ. London Press
Taylor, P. (Edit) 1996 *Researching Drama and Arts Education*, Falmer Press